BECOMING BIBI KAY

KAY OURSLER
AS TOLD TO ROSEMARY J. FISHER

Becoming Bibi Kay
Copyright © 2025 by Kay Oursler

ISBN: 979-8991517997 (sc)

ISBN: 979-8998742408 (e)

Riverview Press

info@riverview-press.com
www.riverview-press.com

Table of Contents

PART ONE
BEGINNING

PART TWO
BECOMING KAY

PART THREE
BECOMING BIBI KAY

PART FOUR
BEING BIBI KAY

Dedication

This book is dedicated to my children,
Jill Sutherland and Jon Oursler,
and their families
and to my African children,
Noel Mgeni, Leida Mgeni,
Shukuru Mgeni, Akiba Mgaya
and Mekio Mwinuka.

**Proceeds from the sale of this book will go to support the
education of Tanzanian orphans.**

Additional copies can be purchased from the authors directly, from
online booksellers, or through Riverview-Press.com.

Kay Oursler – kayhsv1@gmail.com
Rosemary J. Fisher – fisherrosemary72@yahoo.com

About the Author

In many ways, Kay Oursler is your average American woman. She held down jobs as a medical lab technician, in management and in sales, all while raising a family and caring for her home. But in so many other ways, Kay is extraordinary.

Joining the Peace Corps at age sixty-five is highly unusual. Assisting with the building of a dispensary, a library and an orphanage in Africa is exceptional. Giving of her time, finances and compassionate heart make Kay a remarkable woman indeed.

Finally, in 2021, Kay officially retired at the age of eighty-one. But you won't find her sitting still for long! Kay remains active and is always looking for ways to support her African village friends.

Kay returns to her home in Magoda Village, near Njombe, Tanzania, four months out of the year. The rest of her time is split between her mobile home in Mercer, Wisconsin and her apartment in Columbia, Missouri.

While in the United States, Kay enjoys spending time with her daughter, Jill, and son, Jon, and their families. She is active with gardening, relaxes by reading, and plays games at the Senior Center.

And she loves telling stories about her adventures in Africa!

PART ONE
BEGINNING

A New Word in My Vocabulary

This is the story of my life. I'm nobody special, but through a series of events, I have been able to do some very special things. I write this book, not to bring praise or honor to myself, but to share about my adventures and possibly encourage others to look outside themselves, find what skills and gifts they can share with others, and do what they can to make the world a better place.

Every story has a beginning, a middle and an end. Important moments mix with the mundane, one day drifts into several years, and life goes on. Sometimes there are events early in our lives that shape our personalities, our beliefs, and our resilience. These events, probably unnoticed at the time, imbed themselves into our being, form our thought patterns, and create the basis for the people we are to become.

One such event took place in Genoa, Illinois, in 1950, when I was ten years old.

* * * * *

The theater was crowded that afternoon. The matinee showing of Cinderella had drawn in record numbers of Disney fans. Whole families had come, mothers toting toddlers, fathers holding tightly to the hands of young children, and groups of giggling pre-teens under the watchful eye of a parental chaperone. I sold box after box of popcorn and was relieved when the crowd cleared, and the show finally started.

I was boxing up the last of the popcorn when my dad called over from his post at the ticket stand. "Stand up straight, Kay. Stop slouching."

I shifted slightly but answered, "I am standing up straight." I closed the popcorn box and sighed. I had been on my feet, working non-stop, for a couple of hours. I admitted to myself that I was actually slouching a little. But I was tired, maybe that's why.

Dad persisted though and walked over to the popcorn machine. "You are leaning to one side. Can't you straighten up?"

I stood as tall as I could and threw my shoulders back. But I could tell by the look on Dad's face that he wasn't pleased. "Turn around," he said and gently turned me with his big hands. I stood facing the popcorn machine and Dad ran his hand down my back. Slowly he traced my spine from the base of my neck down to my tail bone. Then he did it again.

"Dode," he called over to my mom who was straightening up the ticket booth. "Something is wrong with Kay's back. I'm taking her over to see the new doctor right now." He took me by the hand, and we walked quickly down Main Street. We passed the Post Office and Guse's Groceries. I glanced in the windows of Harry Holroyd Clothing and caught a glimpse of my dad's face in the reflection of the glass. He looked worried. Further down the block we hurried past Fishback's Tavern, Tischler's Grocery, the Huddle Inn, Austin's Shoes and Hayward's Hardware. At the corner we crossed the street and headed to the doctor's office. It was a small building recessed between two bigger buildings.

Doctor Burton had retired, and a new doctor had taken his place. Dad opened the door, and we went into the little waiting room. It was obvious the new doctor hadn't settled his office yet. Boxes of books were stacked almost ceiling high. Odds and ends of furniture were piled in the middle of the room. Apparently, I was about to be his first patient.

"Hello, can I help you?" called a kindly voice from an exam room down the hall. We couldn't see the doctor yet, but he sounded nice.

"Hello, doctor. I'm Fred LeKander. I own the movie theater down the street. I've brought my daughter to see you. I think there's something wrong with her back. She can't stand up straight."

A young man came walking down the hall towards us. He didn't look much like a doctor, dressed in work pants and a plaid shirt. Doctor Burton had always worn a suit and usually had a white coat over the top and a stethoscope around his neck. But I guess this doctor wasn't expecting to actually see patients just yet. He hadn't even unpacked or set up his office.

Even so, he greeted us with a smile and introduced himself. "Welcome! I'm Dr. Carlson." He and Dad shook hands. "As you can see, I'm not really open for business yet." He waved his hand around the lobby indicating the disorganization. "But I'll be glad to take a look. Let's go down to my examination room."

Dad told Dr. Carlson that my spine didn't seem right and together they once again traced the spine from top to bottom. Dr. Carlson asked that I lift my blouse so he could look more closely. I did as I was asked, and in no time at all Dr. Carlson said, "Just as I thought. She has scoliosis."

I didn't know what scoliosis was. I'd never even heard the word before, and I didn't know what it meant. But I was about to learn. I'd have a new word in my vocabulary.

CHAPTER ONE
Let's Start at the Very Beginning

My parents, Dorothy Beach and Fred LeKander, had been married in 1934. Times were hard, being that the country was in a depression. But somehow, my parents, with help from Dad's brother, Glenn, were able to operate a substantial business. Uncle Glenn also ran a theater in Geneva, Illinois and together with my dad and mom, remodeled a building on Main Street in Genoa and installed theater equipment. It was a small theater with only 200 seats, a modest beginning, but Mom and Dad made it work. In 1937, they closed that theater and relocated it in a former old Ford garage. My parents took over running the theater operations and Uncle Glenn went back to Geneva. More remodeling followed and as economic conditions improved in the early 40's, business picked up. People were looking for entertainment, and eager to forget the struggles of the depression years.

I was born in January 1940, and my little brother Dan came along five years later. Our lives were modest yet comfortable. Dad had steady employment, Mom was a wonderful caregiver, and times were simple but good.

Dad had 312 new seats installed in 1949 and built a 'cry room' at the back of the theater. The deep red carpet gave an opulent feeling to the movie-going experience, and the theater drew audiences from far and wide. The theater was fresh and clean, definitely the social hub of Genoa. Yes, the Crystal Theater was the place to be and, even as a young child, I was thrilled to be a part of it.

Dad brought in all the top movies and the theater was a thriving business. Weekends especially brought big crowds, with double features on Friday and Saturday evenings and the matinee on Sunday at 2:00. During the week, the shows were at 7:00. Movie stars like Lana Turner, Laurence Olivier and Roddy McDowell, great dancers like Fred Astair, Ginger Rodgers and Gene Kelley, and wonderful productions like Gone with the Wind and The Greatest Show on Earth filled my early years with fantasy, drama and musical comedy. The Ma and Pa Kettle movies were always a big hit with the local farmers who stood outside the theater and knocked manure off their boots before they walked across our fancy red carpet. Disney movies always sold out fast, and I always got a good seat!

Mom and Dad were a great team and worked together compatibly at whatever they were doing. During the day, Mom stayed home taking care of the house and my little brother, Dan, and me. She always had lunch ready for Dad when he came home from the theater at noon. It was an easy commute for Dad, taking a quick cut through the back alley between the theater and our house.

Dinner was always at 5:05. Afterwards, Dad would take a short twenty-minute nap while Mom and I did the dishes. Then they'd go back to the theater to prepare for the 7:00 show. When Dan and I were young, Mrs. Coonley would watch over us until Mom was able to come back home. Dad always stayed until the last movie had ended and the crowd had emptied out. He was usually home by 10:30 or so, unless he was playing cards with his friends.

Dan and I respected Mrs. Coonley, but kids will be kids and occasionally we pushed a little too hard. If things got out of hand, Mrs. Coonley could always call the theater and speak with Mom or Dad. They were usually able to straighten us out over the phone, but sometimes a face-to-face intervention was necessary. I remember one incident particularly well.

I was eight or nine, and not feeling well. Mom and Dad had gone to work, and Mrs. Coonley was watching over us. Before they left, I had asked Mom if I could have a strawberry sundae from The Huddle Inn. I was sure it would help me feel better. Once she got to the theater, Mom found Happy Overly, who was, as usual, just hanging out at the theater. Happy was practically deaf and to talk to him, we usually wrote him notes or did a little pantomime to act out what we needed. Mom gave Happy some money and wrote him a note asking him to buy a sundae and take it over to the house for me.

When my brother saw that I had ice cream and he didn't, he was mad. In pesky little brother fashion, Dan got a glass of water and poured it all over my bowl of ice cream. Of course, that made me mad, and I slapped him on the back, hard as I could. A lot of crying ensued and try as she might, Mrs. Coonley couldn't get us calmed down. Dan was crying and crying about me hitting him, and I was furious that he had ruined my ice cream. When Mrs. Coonley discovered a bright red mark on Dan's back in the distinct shape of my hand, she called my dad.

Oh boy, was he upset! It was bad enough that his children were out of control, but he had been called away from work, and apparently his daughter had done bodily harm to his son. The evidence was undeniable and, regardless of my reason, hitting my brother was unacceptable. Dad took me by the shoulders, shook me gently for emphasis and said, "Don't you ever do that again." And I never did.

Dad was fun-loving and a little rowdy at times. Maybe that's an understatement. Dad was a hard worker, but he played just as hard. He had a lot of friends and spent many nights hanging out with them after the theater closed, playing poker, smoking and drinking. He took risks too, often when he was too drunk to consider the consequences. I remember hearing about Dad flying a small airplane. That was risky enough, but he did it while he was drinking. The story goes that he flew the plane so low he went under the telephone lines in Genoa. Mom was not happy when she found out.

One night, Dad was playing poker with the guys, totally unaware that bad weather was headed our way. He was concentrating on the game and the streak of winning hands he was playing. As tornado-like winds blew, Mom tried to protect Dan and me by huddling together on a piano bench in the center of the living room, away from windows. It was the best she knew to do. Weather watchers had not yet determined that the safest place to be in a bad storm is in a basement. We didn't know, so we sat there, listening to the wind lash against the house and rain pelt the window as thunder rolled and lightning lit the black sky. It was a very frightening night, made extra scary because Dad wasn't with us.

Dad played on, through the wind and rain, and won big that night. When he finally came home, he was numbed by alcohol and didn't realize that the three of us had been terrified of the storm. All he could think about was the pocketful of cash he had won at the poker table. He stood in the doorway of the living room, scooped money out by the handful and gleefully tossed bills into the air. He was thrilled with his winnings and overjoyed. Mom was not. Sure, she appreciated the money, but she was getting more and more upset with Dad's drinking.

Finally, Dad came to his senses. When I was eight, he quit drinking. He saw how his excessive drinking behavior was making Mom unhappy, so he told her he would quit, and he did. He would do just about anything for my mom. Her happiness was very important to him.

The year I turned ten, while we were eating dinner, Dad looked at Mom and said, "Is it time, Dode?" When Mom nodded, he turned to me and said, "Kay, your mother and I have been talking. We think it's time for you to go to work!"

I sat up a little straighter in my chair, eager to hear what he had to say.

"You know, I've been giving you an allowance for the past few years, but how would you like to make some real money at a real job?"

I was all ears and eager to learn more. The idea of earning my own money was appealing. I was already dreaming about the milkshakes and sundaes I could buy at The Huddle Inn. Dan, my pesky little brother, banged his fork on the table and said, "Me too? I want money too."

"When you are bigger," Mom said calmly. "When you are ten like Kay, then you can come to work at the theater, too. Until then Mrs. Coonley will keep watching you while the rest of us go to work."

Dan wasn't happy about that, but I loved the idea. Dan always wanted to follow me around and he interfered when I had girlfriends over. They didn't mind him; in fact, they said he was adorable. But to me, a five-year-old brother just got in the way. So, a few hours away from him and making money at the same time, well, that was a win-win.

So, my career as popcorn girl began, and I loved it. I was saving up some money, meeting people, making friends, and watching a lot of movies for free, as usual. I was also watching my parents. It was easy to see that they were deeply in love. I could tell they enjoyed working together. Mom was a real support to my dad. She seemed to know just what needed to be done to help the business run smoothly.

Mom was very intelligent. She told me once that she could have been valedictorian of her high school class in Crystal Lake, Illinois, but she was shy and didn't want to give the graduation speech. So, she started purposely failing classes so her grade point would fall, and she wouldn't have to give the speech. She was a problem solver, way back then!

My mother was also beautiful. She was always dressed nicely, with every piece of her dark hair in place and makeup just right. She sold tickets at the front of the lobby, twenty-five cents for adults and fifteen cents for children. Mom always had a smile on her face and a kind word for the customers as they entered the theater.

The movie-goers would then come to me for popcorn, which cost them ten cents for a box. Dad grew his own popcorn, and lots of people said it was the best popcorn in all of DeKalb County, even better than movie popcorn in other theaters. Some people came to the theater just to buy popcorn. I quickly learned how to measure the corn, run the popper and scoop the fluffy buttery morsels into the red and white boxes. I would prepare some boxes before the crowds arrived and have them ready to sell as the first customers came in. Nothing drew people to me faster than the rhythmic sound of bursting kernels and the smell of freshly popped corn, and I kept the popper popping!

Dad took tickets at a little podium. He'd tear the ticket in half and push the pieces into a trash slot as he welcomed people to the show. He was a tall, good-looking man, with an easy laugh and a handsome smile. He was a hard worker, too, and always found ways to provide for his family. He adored my mother and was quick to show affection. They never parted without a goodbye kiss.

Crystal Theater - 1955

When I started working at the theater, at age ten, only a few of my friends had actual jobs, and none of them were as glamorous as mine. Most of my classmates de-tasseled corn in the summer and were busy with farm chores all year round. I realized how fortunate I was. I watched so many good movies that summer. Many were Academy Award winners. I always kept up on the stars and lived vicariously through their lives on the big screen. I once watched a movie that made me cry uncontrollably. When I came out of the theater to return to the popcorn machine, my eyes were red and swollen. Dad got someone else to sell the popcorn and sent me home to recover. After an hour or so, I was more presentable and returned to my job.

My life was full. I had lots of friends and a job I enjoyed. My dad bought me a pony and I even had a lamb for a pet. We kept them in a red barn at the back end of our property.

Our backyard was a paradise. Mom and Dad had worked hard together, making the most beautiful setting possible. Lilac bushes lined one side of the yard, with peonies planted in front. There were iris, daffodils and other flowers, too. The opposite side of the yard had grapes growing on a fence. Dad had built a purple martin house that stood high on a pole in the center of the yard. He kept that yard looking beautiful, with bushes trimmed and grass mowed.

A gate separated the yard from our vegetable garden. Dad's favorite thing to grow was horseradish. He loved the taste and put a little horseradish on everything.

Just past the little garden was the red barn for my pony. I loved to play with that pony. Dad rigged up a little cart and that pony would give us rides around the neighborhood.

We had great neighbors, too. In a small town, everybody knows everybody. Often in the evenings, people would walk around the neighborhood, stopping to chat with others who were gathered on their front porches or tending their flower beds.

Across the alley and on the corner near the theater, there was a green house. Mrs. Zula Roush lived there. She was an elderly lady, quite the neighborhood character. She had a laugh that could be heard for blocks. I could even hear her laughing from inside my bedroom. Once she was laughing and cackling and carrying on so, I went over to see what was so funny. In an empty lot beside her house, Zula Roush kept chickens. I watched as she grabbed a chicken by the head and swung it around until the neck was broken. Then she twisted the neck bones until she could pull the head completely off that chicken. Still laughing loudly, she watched as the chicken body ran around, headless but still alive for a few minutes. I had to admit, even though it was both horrifying and sad, it was pretty funny too!

Life in our little town was comfortable. We weren't rich as far as money goes, but we managed to get by. I had a well-respected family, enough to eat, and felt safe and loved. As much as a ten-year-old thinks about the future, I figured I had a great life to look forward to.

That all changed when I heard the word scoliosis. Suddenly the future seemed uncertain.

CHAPTER TWO

Summer 1950

My job at the theater was so much fun. I loved the bustle of activity, the delicious smell of popcorn and the constant flow of people all around. When the shows started and the lobby wasn't crowded, I cleaned up my popcorn area and prepared for the next group of movie-goers. I felt like I was part of an exciting world – movies, stars, friends, good times. Being in the theater made me happy.

Working with my mom and dad also brought me happiness. I was helping our family and the business. And I was making some money that was all my own. It was a good feeling. Other kids my age were working for their families too, doing dirty, sweaty farm work. My job was glamourous by comparison. And I got to watch whatever movies I wanted!

For a young girl of ten, I figured my life was pretty good. I liked school and was better than the average student. I had many friends, and my days were filled with giggles and good times. We played outside until dark riding bikes, climbing trees and catching lightning bugs. We never worried about strangers or crime. Nobody locked their doors or cars. We trusted our neighbors and knew everybody in town. I had what I considered a dream job and was happy to be helping in the family business. For the most part, I lived in the carefree dream world of a ten-year-old. Most of my worries centered around math quizzes, spelling tests, and my pesky little brother.

The day Dad walked me through town towards the doctor's office, I had no idea how my safe and comfortable little world was going to change. I could tell Dad thought there was a problem. That concerned me, but I still didn't know what it all meant.

When I heard Dr. Carlson say the word 'scoliosis,' my trouble-free life suddenly took on an aura of uncertainty. It was a big word, foreign to me as well as to my parents. We had a lot of questions. I could tell, without being told, that it wasn't a good thing. I had no idea just how it would affect my future.

I didn't know Dr. Carlson. He was new in town and was taking over Dr. Burton's practice. He wasn't even ready to see patients yet; we had to walk past boxes and piles of books just to get into his exam room. But he was kind and gentle. And Dad seemed to trust him.

After Dr Carlson looked at my back and studied my spine, he looked at my dad and said those foreign words. "She has scoliosis." And my life changed, just like that. Suddenly there was a dark cloud hanging over me. Actually, that cloud hung over my whole family. We were all affected by the diagnosis.

Dad and I held hands as we walked back to the theater and got there just before the movie ended. Dad hurriedly gave the news to Mom and said Dr. Carlson wanted to see us all in his office the next day. Mom gave me a quick hug and said, "Don't you worry, Kay. We'll take care of this. You'll be fine."

I walked back to my popcorn stand, wondering if Mom really believed what she said or was just trying to convince herself. The lobby filled with people exiting the theater, and my parents and I got busy preparing for the next show. Every once in a while, I noticed Mom look over at Dad and he gave her a smile of reassurance.

Still not knowing what lay ahead, I tried to find comfort in the normalcy of popping corn. Whatever the future held, worrying about it wouldn't change a thing. So, I busied myself with the routines around me and determined to take it one day at a time.

CHAPTER THREE
Diagnosis

In Dr. Carlson's office the next day, we gathered to learn more about this diagnosis. Dr. Carlson had been busy unpacking, and it was easier to walk through the waiting room. Most of the boxes had been emptied, and the bookshelves were filled with big fat medical journals. Dr. Carlson sat behind the desk in his office. Mom and Dad sat opposite him, one on either side of me.

"Scoliosis is a curvature of the spine. Nobody really knows why it happens; It might be because of an accident, or hereditary, or a birth defect. Or it can be a combination of everything or none of those at all. We don't completely know."

Mom gave a little shudder and Dad leaned closer to the desk. "But can you fix it?" he asked hopefully.

"Minor cases can be helped with a corset or brace and exercises, but Kay's case doesn't seem to be minor. She will require surgery, and I am not qualified to do it. Fortunately, one of the foremost surgeons in scoliosis correction is in Chicago. His name is Dr. Claude Lambert, and he works out of St. Luke's Presbyterian Hospital. If you'd like, I will call him and explain Kay's case. I'll let you know when he can see Kay, and we'll go from there."

The walk home was somber. Surgery was a big, ominous word for a little girl of ten. My head was spinning with questions, most of which I was afraid to ask. Would it hurt? Would I miss school? What if I didn't have the surgery?

I listened as Mom and Dad talked. Mom had questions, too. "I wonder what this surgery involves. Working on the spine sounds risky."

Dad was quick to silence her fears. "Calm down, Dode. It's going to work out alright. Let's go see this Doctor Lambert. It sounds like he will know what's best. Apparently, he's an expert. Kay will be in good hands."

So, Dad drove me to Chicago for our first appointment. It took about two hours to get to the city and most of the ride was spent in silence. I guess Dad was concentrating on driving in the big city. And I was deep in thought, or more correctly, trying *not* to think.

St. Luke's Presbyterian Hospital was an impressive looking building. Made of red brick and standing six stories high, it was probably the biggest building I had ever been in. We walked between two cement columns and through a recessed courtyard to reach the tall double doors. Inside the lobby we were directed to an exam room where a nurse wrote down some information on a chart. She gave me a gray hospital gown and asked me to change out of my clothes. "Keep it open in the back," she said. "Dr. Lambert will want to see how your spine looks."

Dad left the room, and I dressed myself in a gray hospital gown. I hung my clothes up on a hook on the wall. The gown was loose fitting and went all the way down to my feet. They probably didn't have any child-sized gowns, I figured. I tied it around the neck and sat down on the little bed. The gown was open in the back, and I felt a draft.

There was a knock at the door and Dad and Dr. Lambert came in. Dressed in suit pants and a white shirt, Dr. Lambert had a cigarette hanging from his lips. He wore a long white coat over his clothes and had a stethoscope around his neck. He put the cigarette in an ashtray on the counter, and it burned throughout the exam. The smell of the smoke tickled my throat.

Several younger doctors came in, too. Dr. Lambert motioned for them to gather around the examination bed. The room was very crowded, and I felt all eyes looking at me. "Kay, I'm Dr. Lambert and these young men are doctors studying to learn more about cases like yours. I'm going to examine your back, and they will be watching. Let's begin."

As I sat on the bed, Dr. Lambert opened the back of my gown. The young doctors looked on as he ran his hand down my spine, tracing the curve of the bones. He instructed each of the younger men to also feel my back, and one by one they leaned over me, prodding and poking at my bones. Occasionally, one would mumble, "Ahh, I see!" or "My, oh my!" I felt like I was not a person, just part of a science lesson.

Dr. Lambert asked me to stand up as straight as I could. He took a metal rod and placed it on my back; then I felt him slide a piece of paper under the rod and draw the curve of my spine. He passed the paper around so all the young doctors could see.

When each man had taken a turn, Dr. Lambert turned to one and asked, "What is your evaluation, Dr. Adamson?"

"Scoliosis, greater than fifty degrees. This is a severe case."

"Correct," said Dr. Lambert. He turned to another young man and asked, "And Dr. Martin, what would be your recommendation?"

Dr. Martin stuttered and seemed unsure of himself as he said, "Surgery is recommended. Otherwise, she'll grow a hunchback."

Another man waved his hand and interrupted. "But sir, I would not recommend surgery for this young lady until she is older, maybe thirteen. Her bones are still growing. If we did surgery now, it would have to be re-done in five years or so. I advise waiting."

"Thank you, Dr. Benson. I agree." Dr. Lambert turned to another young man and asked, "Dr. Kilpatrick, do you have any recommendations for her as we wait for a more appropriate time for surgery?"

Dr. Kilpatrick pushed his black glasses up on his nose and answered. "First, I'd like to listen to her lungs and judge her breathing capacity." He turned to me and asked, "May I?" When I nodded, he put his stethoscope on my back and asked me to breathe deeply. Then he listened in the front too.

"Her lungs do seem slightly compromised. The curvature inhibits full lung capacity. I would recommend deep breathing exercises. And I would suggest she take up a wind instrument, such as a clarinet or trumpet, to increase oxygen flow."

Dr. Lambert smiled and made a note on his clipboard. "Excellent, Dr. Kilpatrick. Well done!" Dr. Kilpatrick seemed pleased with the compliment. He squared his shoulders and stood a little taller.

Not to be outdone, Dr. Martin jumped in with his own recommendation. "I suggest increasing calcium intake and get plenty of rest."

"Yes, that's good." Dr. Lambert wrote some notes on paper and handed it to my dad. "We'll want to see her back in six months for a re-examination and then every six months there-after. We'll take measurements each time, see how quickly she's digressing. When she is twelve or thirteen, we will discuss the surgical procedure. In the meantime, follow the recommendations of these fine young men."

Dr. Lambert reached for his cigarette, took one puff and stubbed it out in the ashtray. He turned back to my dad and went down the list of recommendations. "More milk, start woodwind lessons, and at least an hour of rest, flat on her back, every afternoon after school."

The young doctors filed out of the room. Before he left, the one named Dr. Kilpatrick turned and said to me, "It was a pleasure to meet you, Kay. And don't you worry; Dr. Lambert is the best in the business. He'll fix you up and you'll be standing tall and straight in no time."

When the men were gone and the door was closed, Dr. Lambert turned to my dad. "Do you have any questions?" he asked.

"This surgery…." Dad began. "It's necessary? She won't get better without it?"

"It's imperative," he answered. "She *won't* get better, but she *will* get worse. Surgery is her only hope of a normal life." Dr. Lambert was adamant. Surgery was required.

I didn't understand completely, but my eyes filled with tears. I squeezed them tight, so Dad didn't see. I turned to take my clothes off the hook. But mostly I was trying to hide my tears from Dad.

CHAPTER FOUR
Treatment Begins

We made trips to Chicago every six months for two years. Each time the curve seemed to be getting worse. Each time a new group of young doctors gave their opinions and Dr. Lambert either agreed or corrected them. Each time I felt like a lab rat, but I came to take it all as a matter of fact. Once my body started changing and becoming more womanly, however, I felt more self-conscious about men looking at me. 'But they're doctors,' I kept telling myself, and I tried not to think about them checking out my maturing body.

I followed the doctor's orders. In fifth grade, I started taking clarinet lessons from our music teacher Mr. Hubbell. I also played the flute -a -phone, a little plastic instrument that was like a clarinet but much smaller. It was so much fun to play, and I could take it with me anywhere.

I also drank a lot of milk and ate a lot of ice cream. It was easy to go uptown to The Huddle Inn with my money from the theater and get a sundae or a milkshake. I felt like I was taking care of my bones and the more ice cream the better.

Resting every day, though, flat on my back, that wasn't much fun. Staring at the ceiling, listening to my brother play or kids riding bikes past our house, was frustrating. I wanted to be up and around, chatting with my girlfriends or playing with my pony. But hard as it was, I did what was expected of me.

I loved my fifth-grade teacher Mrs. Geraldine Clucus– everyone did. She was a brand-new teacher, and we were her very first class. She had energy and a personality that made school fun. I was a good student and enjoyed school. One of my report cards said I was 'a very good student but lacked self-confidence.'

During sixth and seventh grade, my life was pretty normal. I went to school, kept up with my clarinet lessons and giggled with my girlfriends. I made popcorn at the theater, watched a lot of movies, and tolerated my little brother. I did my homework, helped with housework and obeyed my parents, usually. Meanwhile, I practiced deep breathing exercises, stared at the ceiling for an hour every day, and prayed for the day this ordeal would be behind me.

Church attendance was important to my parents, although they didn't usually go themselves, except for religious holidays. Mom and Dad worked late at the theater on Saturday nights and then would often spend time with friends. Dad and Jack Cooper and Mr. Aken were in a band of sorts. They would get together at our house late on Saturday evenings, having jam sessions. Dad played the drums. So, Mom and Dad were usually up really late on Saturday evenings. Because they had to be ready for the Sunday afternoon matinee, they felt that Sunday morning was the only chance they had to catch up on their sleep. But they made sure I went to church, and they made sure I had money for the offering plate. One year I got a perfect attendance award for Sunday school.

CHAPTER FIVE

Hospital Stay

Finally, the day came. In the fall of my eighth-grade year, 1953, Dr. Lambert decided that it was time for surgery. In December, Mom and Dad took me to St. Luke's Hospital and the procedure began. I could never have been prepared for what happened to me next!

I was wrapped in a plaster of Paris cast from my chin, down my torso, past my waist. The cast went down my left leg to my knee but on my right side it stopped at my hip. I felt like a mummy. I couldn't turn my head; I couldn't move anything but my arms. I was stuck. I was placed in a hospital bed, on my back, and that's pretty much how I stayed for the next 10 days.

Someone had to feed me. Someone had to lift me carefully onto a bedpan. I was helpless. I couldn't roll over, couldn't sit up, couldn't do anything but lay there hour after hour.

I was in a children's ward with seven beds besides mine. Most of the kids in the ward had just had their tonsils taken out. They stayed a couple of days and then got to go home. I seemed to be the only long-termer.

I couldn't even see the other kids. I was just aware that beds were moving in and out as they came and went. I was also aware of the smell of ether that seemed to fill the room every time a new kid came in from surgery. It was a horrible nauseating smell and made my stay in the ward that much more difficult.

A mother of one of the tonsillectomy patients took pity on me. She would come and sit beside my bed and hold my hand. She was a black woman, and the sweetest lady. She would sing and pray and talk to me about Jesus. It certainly helped to pass the time, for a couple of days, and I appreciated her comforting presence.

Mom and Dad could only come to visit me twice. It was a long trip, and they needed to stay home and keep the theater going. So, most of the time I was alone. I did understand that they needed to be at the theater, and I knew it was important. But at the same time, I really missed them and sometimes cried out of loneliness.

I did talk to my parents on the phone a few times. One of the nurses would bring the telephone to me. I could hold it up to my ear while I lay on my back to talk. It was good to hear about what was happening at home. Even talking to my brother, Dan, could lift my spirits a little.

Once, Dad asked me if there was anything I needed. He was surprised when I told him what I really wanted was a dill pickle. But a few days later, I was the one who was surprised. Our neighbor, Helen Campbell, had come to visit me in the hospital. I was really excited to have a visitor, and even more thrilled when she pulled a dill pickle out of her pocketbook! She unwrapped the pickle and held it up to my lips. It was a real treat – the best thing I had eaten in a long time. I will forever be thankful for Helen and her dill pickle!

Someone figured out a way to rig up some glasses with mirrors at an angle so I could look out the window. I don't know how they did it, but I could lie on my back, put on these fancy glasses, and somehow see the sky and an American flag fluttering in the breeze. It wasn't much but was sure better than counting cracks in the ceiling plaster.

Using those glasses, I could also read comic books. It was hard, since I had to stay on my back and hold the comic book over my face, but it did help to pass the time a little.

Besides being homesick and lonely, laying there day in and day out, I was in pain. Every day, someone would come in and tighten the cast that had a turnbuckle. They were trying to force my spine to line up straighter. I dreaded it, and it left me in pain so much that I would cry. I wanted to scream out loud but tried hard not to embarrass myself by crying too much. I couldn't help myself sometimes – it really hurt! I suppose the tonsillectomy kids thought I was a baby, but they didn't have to go through the pain I did. It was terrible, and I was beginning to wonder if it was worth it.

Finally, after ten days in the plaster cast, I was taken into a small room and gently rolled onto my side. A large square section of the cast on my back was cut out so Dr. Lambert could work on my spine. Then I was rolled into the operating room for the actual surgery. Now it was my turn to go under the ether. The room was filled with people. There were several nurses assisting Dr. Lambert. In addition, some young doctors were there to observe as well. Dr. Lambert stood near my shoulder and explained about breathing the ether and drifting off to sleep. I was thankful that he didn't have a cigarette in the operating room with him. That was my last thought before I lost consciousness.

Next thing I knew, several hours had passed and I was waking up in the recovery room. My parents were with me, and nurses were hovering over me, charting my vitals as I came back from my sleep. Mom held my hand and spoke soothingly to me. Dad stood behind her with his hands on her shoulders.

"You made it," he said to me. "You're going to be fine."

"I don't feel so fine," I said, "I have a headache." I moaned and covered my eyes with my hand. I struggled and Dad stepped close.

"Easy, Kay, easy. You must be still."

A nurse came in and gave me a shot in my rump. "It's penicillin," she said when Mom asked what it was. "It will keep away infection."

The shot didn't hurt me, but it made me feel strange. It was like I could feel the medicine going all through my body. I didn't like it, but feeling so groggy as I was, I drifted off to sleep. When I woke more fully, I was back in the children's ward. Mom and Dad were sitting in chairs next to my bed.

"Kay, can you eat a little something?" Mom asked. "Dad and I have to leave soon; it's getting late. But I want to help you eat, if you can, before we go." I didn't have much of an appetite; the smell of ether lingered in my throat. But I ate a few bites of the soup she fed me and a cracker. It was enough to satisfy her, I guess, because a few minutes later she leaned over me, kissed my forehead and put on her coat. "We'll talk on the phone soon," she said as she turned to leave. There was a little catch in her voice, and I wondered if she was crying.

Dad squeezed my hand and said, "You be a good girl. Listen to Dr. Lambert and do what he says. We'll be back in a week or so to take you home."

I slept fitfully that night and as the ether wore off completely, I became more aware of the pain. I was lying on my back, right on top of the surgical area. And my left leg hurt a lot. When the nurse came in the next morning, she spent a lot of time working on my leg. I couldn't really see it, so I asked what she was doing.

"Just checking your incision and changing the bandages." She lifted the leg carefully and wrapped a gauze bandage around it.

"What happened to my leg?" I was confused. "I was supposed to have the surgery on my back. Why is my leg bandaged?"

"Dr Lambert took some bone from your leg and used it to fuse into your spine. That leg bone material will help your spine grow strong and straight."

"But my leg!" I exclaimed. "How will I walk without a leg?" I was in a panic.

The nurse patted my hand comfortingly and said, "Oh, Kay, you will be just fine. Dr. Lambert didn't take your whole leg, just some of the bone, and it will grow back. The human body is an amazing thing. You will be able to run and jump in no time. Your spine will be straighter, and your leg will be stronger. You'll see."

I gave a little sigh of relief and tried to relax. But then she said something that bothered me even more. "Dr. Lambert wants you to use the bedpan and have a bowel movement. Do you think you can do that for me today? I see on your chart you haven't had a movement the whole time you have been here. That's nearly two weeks! We can't let you go home until you've had a normal movement."

I wanted to shake my head no, but I couldn't move it. So, I just scrunched up my face in protest. "I don't think I want to," I said. I thought it would be so embarrassing. Using the bedpan for pee was bad enough, but I was not about to poop in a pan! No way!

"Well, Dr. Lambert says it's important. You're going to have to, and soon." The nurse went about her business, and I just closed my eyes. I thought that would be the end of the conversation, and she would just go away. But there was more torture coming my way.

"Time for your penicillin shot," she said, and my eyes flew open.

It was even worse than I remembered from the shot the day before. As the medicine coursed through my body, a wave of nausea came over me. Soon I could feel the penicillin in every part of my legs and arms. I didn't like it, not one bit.

The nurse left and I lay very still in my bed. It took a while for the horrible feeling to lesson. I wondered how many more of those shots I was going to get.

The days crawled by. I was quite bored. I listened to the other children in the ward, chatting with each other, moving around on their beds, receiving visitors. The only people who came to see me were doctors, nurses and people learning to be doctors and nurses. Everyone was kind, but they were all busy and couldn't spend a lot of time with me. I was anxious to go home, yet unsure of how that was going to happen.

One of the student nurses was young and pretty. She did take the time to sit and talk with me whenever she could. I felt like she was really trying to show some sympathy to me in my uncomfortable condition. She seemed sensitive to my misery. I liked her bedside manner and felt like she was going to make a great nurse.

By the fifth day, I had decided that I didn't want any more penicillin shots. Every shot made me feel creepy. Each felt worse than the one before. When the nurse came in to give me another shot, I refused. I guess Dr. Lambert agreed that I had had enough of the antibiotic because he didn't force the issue.

One issue he did force was the bedpan. I'd been in the hospital almost three weeks without a bowel movement and Dr. Lambert was not happy. He sent one of the other doctors in to deliver the ultimatum. That young doctor stood at the side of my bed and had a serious conversation with me. "Young lady, you must have a bowel movement. It's not good to get all clogged up, you know." He raised up his hand and wiggled his pointy finger. "And if you don't go on your own, I'm going to have to go up in there and clean you out myself." He said it in a threatening way, but he was smiling too. I guess he thought that would be enough to get things moving, but he was wrong.

There was no way I was going to go in the bedpan. The next day, Dr. Lambert came to my bed and said I would be going home that afternoon. He had called my parents and explained the situation. They all thought I might feel more comfortable using the pan at home, so Dr. Lambert agreed to discharge me. A few hours later, here came my dad and Jack Cooper. Jack was the Genoa undertaker, and he had an ambulance! I rode all the way home in that ambulance, rotated slightly on my side so I could watch out the window. The big buildings of the city gave way to residential neighborhoods and soon we were in a more rural area. It was the first time I had seen the countryside in more than three weeks. Dad sat back there with me and kept me calm. Bumps in the road jolted me but I tried not to complain. I was going home!

CHAPTER SIX

Recovery

Things were different at home. I couldn't go to my bedroom upstairs, of course, so Mom had rearranged things. She and Dad had moved their bed into the den and a hospital bed was set up for me in their room. I got home from the hospital just in time to celebrate my fourteenth birthday. It was certainly a unique celebration, eating cake and ice cream lying in bed on my side. At least I was able to feed myself now. I was thankful for that.

I spent the next three months in that hospital bed. I was on my back a lot, but I was also allowed to lie on my side. I just couldn't roll myself over, so I always had to ask for help. My mother was so patient and kind. I never heard her mumble about how much extra work she had to do for me. She never complained about helping me on and off the bedpan. She smiled as she rolled me gently from side to side to change the sheets on my bed. Not once did she seem unhappy about caring for me. She did everything she could to make my days more pleasant.

The cast was uncomfortable, as you can probably imagine. Over time it began to rub on my chin and my armpits, causing pressure points that were red and raw. Mom brought some hot pads to cushion my arms and a cloth to protect my chin, so the cast didn't irritate the skin as much.

In bed with my pets

Our dog, Pug, was a loyal companion during this time. She was a cute little black and white Boston terrier, and I think she missed me while I was in the hospital. Once I got home, she seldom left my side. She would often jump up on my bed and cuddle with me. I liked her companionship.

I also loved having human company! My classmates came and visited me almost every day. I loved it when my best girlfriends just came over to talk. Even though I was 'different' because of my cast and my limitations, they always made me feel included and never left me out. We would talk and giggle just like always. We laughed so hard when young Jackie Hodgson entertained us with her silly cheerleading routines. She was a great distraction, with her singing and dancing and fooling around.

Sometimes they brought me gifts. My classmates went together and bought me a parakeet! I named him Jimmy, and it was fun to watch as he hopped around his cage which was set near my bed. I got presents from people in the neighborhood, too. Perfume, pajamas, books, and treats. All in all, I received fifty-two gifts from people in town. I no longer felt forgotten or isolated. Those three lonely weeks in the Chicago hospital became a distant memory.

Dad did what he could to help me pass the time more comfortably. One day he really surprised me. I heard a lot of commotion in the living room and when Dad came into the bedroom, I couldn't believe my eyes. He was pushing a little table into the room, and on top of the table was a small television set. Dad thought having a television to watch might help me enjoy my confinement just a little.

One thing I knew about my dad – he detested television. He believed (and rightly so) that if families had televisions in their homes, they would be less likely to go to the movies. He feared that television would bring about the ruin of his theater business. But here he was, bringing in a television for me, his daughter, to help me through the lonely hours of my recovery from surgery. I know that was difficult for dad, but he did it for me.

And I did enjoy it! I liked watching Kukla, Fran and Ollie, Roy Rogers, and Howdy Doody. The 'I Love Lucy' show made me laugh and laugh. Even though the shows were in black and white and often looked like snow, the television still brought me great pleasure and entertained me.

Whenever I was done watching or when visitors came over, Mom or Dad would move the television into a closet, so no one knew we had it. It stayed hidden until all the visitors left the house. It wouldn't be right for the theater owners to promote television watching!

My eighth-grade teachers came every couple of days to go over schoolwork with me. Mrs. Soli and Mrs. Baker made sure I didn't fall behind. I was able to write a little while lying on my side, so I did worksheets and even took exams, all from the comfort of my hospital bed.

Another visitor I had was a real surprise. I had been confined to my bed for almost three months. It was near the end of eighth grade. All my friends were excited about the end of the school year, but I just couldn't get happy about it. I was still stuck in this bed, sweating in the heat and wishing I could get out of that awful body cast. That's when Dr. Lambert came all the way from Chicago on a Sunday afternoon to check on me. He even brought his wife along. Dr. Lambert took my hand and looked proudly into my eyes. "Your mother told me the good news," he said.

I wasn't sure what he was talking about, so I asked, "What news do you mean?"

He leaned closer to me and whispered, loud enough for everyone to hear, "You've had bowel movements in the bedpan! I knew you could do it!"

Mom and Dad chuckled but I was embarrassed! But not as embarrassed as I would have been doing that in the hospital. So, I changed the subject, fast.

"I wish my skin didn't itch so much." I said.

Dad picked up the conversation. "Can you do anything about her itching?" he asked. "Her skin is so dry and flaky, under that cast. She tells me all the time she wants to scratch it."

Dr. Lambert looked at me and asked, "Where does it itch?"

34

"Everywhere! My back, my shoulders, my tummy, even my leg. I just itch all over. And it's hot," I added.

In no time, Dr. Lambert had cut a circle shape in the cast on my stomach area. As soon as he did, a breeze cooled my belly. I felt better instantly. He told my mom to find a corset stay to use as a scratcher. She went looking through her closet, chatting with Mrs. Lambert while searching for my grandma's old corset. Pretty soon she found it and removed a long thin piece of bone. "This should work," she said, and Mrs. Lambert nodded in agreement.

Dr. Lambert took the stay and inserted it into the hole in the cast. He showed me how to move it around to find the itchy spots. Then he put it inside my armhole opening and also down my back. It really felt better. I was getting some relief.

Dad and Dr. Lambert lit up cigarettes and went out into the kitchen to talk some more. The women joined them, and I heard Mom pouring coffee for everyone. The Lamberts stayed quite a while, and I drifted off to sleep. I couldn't hear them talking, and I couldn't watch television, so I just closed my eyes.

Next thing I knew, Dr. Lambert was saying goodbye. He patted me on the shoulder and said, "Kay, I was just telling your mom and dad that Dr. Carlson will be by in a few days to check on your leg incision. It looks like he'll be able to cut your cast soon, so both sides will match. That will help with the itching, too."

I smiled my thanks, and the Lamberts left. Mom came into my room and sat on the bed, looking at me lovingly. "You are doing so well, Kay. I'm sure this hasn't been much fun, but you are getting better every day and soon this will all be behind you. And you will have a great story to tell."

At that point in my life, I didn't really care about having a story to tell. I just wanted everything to get back to normal. The end of eighth grade was right around the corner and I was wondering if

I could go to graduation. I got the answer to that question a few days later, when Dr. Carlson came to cut the cast from my left leg.

Once my leg was free, I was able to practice walking. I was wobbly and unsteady at first; after all, I had been on my back for four months. My legs were weak, and I was very cautious. I felt like a turtle, covered in a shell from head to legs. Carrying that plaster around wasn't easy. It was heavy and so restrictive. Dr Carlson warned me, "Now don't you do any cartwheels, young lady." I laughed but realized I did have to be very careful. I certainly didn't want to fall and break anything.

Before long, it was the afternoon of eighth grade graduation. I walked in with my class and sat up tall and straight in the auditorium chairs. When it was my turn to receive my diploma, my classmates clapped extra loud in support of my accomplishment. It hadn't been easy, and certainly wasn't the normal way to spend eighth grade. But I had done it, with the help of my doctors, my parents, my friends and teachers, and the whole community.

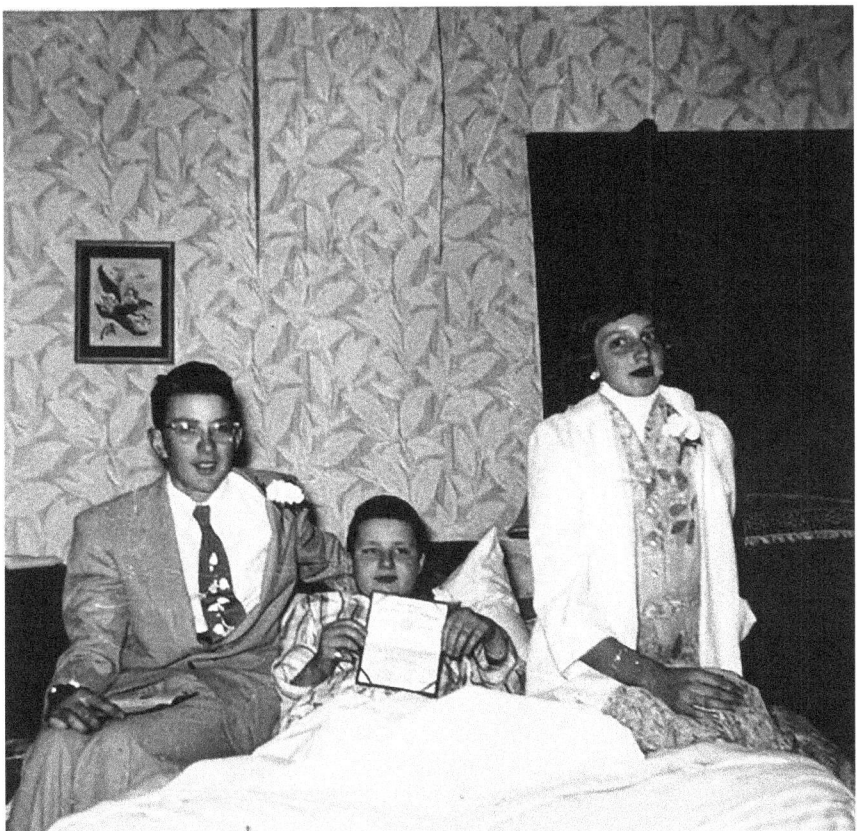

Celebrating 8th grade graduation with my date Dick Fowler and our friend Bob Campbell. (Bob was in bed with a head injury – someone accidentally hit him in the head with a baseball bat!)

All that summer, I still wore my cast. It stretched from my chin to my hips, but now there was a change. Dr. Carlson told me that Dr. Lambert said it was time to cut down the neckline of the cast, so my chin no longer had to rest on it. He also informed me that the cast would be modified so that I could take it off and on. A cut was made under my right arm and all the way down. They put a hinge on it, so it could be opened. Freedom! Well, at least a little!

I was allowed to take the cast off for a couple of hours each day. When school started in the fall, I wore the cast all day and removed it when I got home. After dinner I would put it back on. Eventually I was allowed to sleep without the cast.

In December of my ninth-grade year, the cast was permanently removed. I had worn it for almost eleven whole months.

Dr. Lambert was very satisfied with the results of my surgery. The curvature of my spine had been corrected from nearly seventy degrees to a mere twenty. My prognosis was good. I was expected to live a normal life. According to Dr. Lambert, I had only two restrictions. "No heavy lifting and no jack-knife dives," he said.

I laughed and said, "No problem! I don't know how to do jack-knife dives anyway!"

CHAPTER SEVEN
In Summary

I will forever be grateful for the doctors and nurses who cared for me. Even the medical students influenced my life. I give thanks for the support of my friends, teachers and other community members who stood with me through those difficult days. And my parents – my dad who insisted on the best care available at the time and my mom, who never complained one bit during my recovery.

Back in the 1950's a diagnosis of scoliosis was a frightening thing. Modern medicine has come so far! X-Rays and MRIs can pinpoint the exact degree of curvature. Medical procedures and sanitary environments have made surgery safer and more predictable. A variety of pain medications can be safely given. Knowledge of the human body and how it repairs itself has increased the number of positive outcomes.

Because we understand the skeletal system better now than we did seventy-five years ago, a scoliosis diagnosis today does not come with a high level of fear or uncertainty. Trained surgeons have years of case studies to learn from and, using the information they gather from their knowledge of past procedures and successes, they can proceed with confidence. New surgery procedures involving insertion of metal rods have been very successful. The reality is, scoliosis is not curable at this time, but it is treatable. And the future for a scoliosis patient is positive and bright.

I am in my eighties now and am happy to report that my back has never given me a significant problem through all my adult years. In my twenties, when my two children were born, I did have intense back pain during contractions, which was probably due to the extra pressure on my spine. But other than that, I hardly ever knew there had been an issue. I did learn that the blood transfusions I received during surgery had been contaminated, and I tested positive for Hepatitis C in the 1980's when I gave blood at the Red Cross. It was something I would have to watch for the rest of my life, but it hasn't caused me any physical trouble. My life has not been restricted because of my scoliosis. I can walk and ride a bike. I've slept on hard floors and (don't tell Dr. Lambert) I've carried heavy loads. I helped with construction projects, painting and laying tile. I've planted gardens and harvested wheat. I climbed ladders and hiked mountain trails in the Grand Canyon. My life has been full.

The only thing I can't do is a jack-knife dive.

PART TWO
BECOMING KAY

Stages

Day by day, year by year, time marches on. Soon I found myself immersed in high school, college and marriage. Balancing family and work, maneuvering happiness and tears, working through dreams and disappointments, I was becoming the adult version of myself.

Just as an infant develops one stage at a time, so too the adult life is built upon experiences and levels of growth. My adult years were like many of my contemporaries: graduation, college, marriage and employment. Yet there were events in my life that molded me into the woman I became, a woman with vision, drive, independence and determination. Those characteristics, forged in happy memories and shattered dreams, laid the foundation for the Kay I would become. And they would carry me through my entire adult life.

CHAPTER ONE
High School

The halls of Genoa-Kingston High were bustling with students happy to be together again after summer break. School had only been in session for a few days, and kids were still greeting each other like long lost friends. A joyful excitement could be felt. The semester was new; homework, term papers and extra credit work hadn't even been discussed yet. All that would come, I was sure; it always did. But today, there were no worries about grades or tests.

As I walked to class with my friends Donna and Carol, I could hardly believe what had just happened. We had just come from our first freshman class meeting, and I had been nominated to be class president! I never would have expected that! Just a few years ago, my teacher had written on my report card that I lacked confidence. And now, here I was, running for a position of leadership at school. Quite the surprise.

I settled into my seat and tried to get comfortable. I was still wearing my cast at school, which meant I had to sit up very straight in my chair. No slouching during class, that's for sure! I walked tall and straight, too. I couldn't do otherwise; the cast kept my back erect all the time.

Dick Fowler walked past my desk and stopped to talk before the bell rang. "I know how you can win the election," he said. "Offer free popcorn at the theater to anyone who votes for you!" He thought it was funny. I just rolled my eyes and shook my head. If that was the way I was going to get votes, I didn't want the job.

Walking home with Barbara and Bob after school that day, I got to wondering why I had been nominated. I was kind of popular, but I was surprised that anyone would think I could be president. Even though I was a little shy, I probably could be a good class president. After all, how hard could it be? But I wasn't going to bribe anyone to vote for me. I wasn't going to use bribery to get ahead.

Bob said, "Kay, you have lots of friends. Everybody knows you. Everybody likes you. You even walk like a queen. You must be president. It suits you!"

My Queenly posture

We laughed as we walked along. "I don't have a choice, you know. I have to walk tall and straight because of this cast!"

Barbara straightened her back, held her head high and walked like royalty. "Maybe I could have been nominated if I walked like a queen too!"

Bob bowed low before us and said, "Your majesties! I, Sir Robert, am here to do your bidding!" Barbara and I burst into fits of giggles.

When the laughter died down, I said, "The election is next week. I really think Roy Lilly will win. He's more president material."

"No, you will win. Everyone will want to show you how much they care about all the pain you've gone through in the last year. They'll vote for you to make you feel good." Barbara said what I had been thinking.

I don't know if that was the reason or not, but the next week I was elected class president and it turned out to be fun. I did a pretty good job of leading our class for freshman year.

In December, I went back to St. Luke's Presbyterian Hospital in Chicago to meet with Dr. Lambert one last time. He was very pleased with the results of the surgery and said the cast could be permanently removed. He said our local doctor could follow my progress, but he expected I would be just fine.

And he was right.

When Sophomore year resumed after summer break, I asked Roy Lilly what had kept him busy all summer. I was dumbfounded to hear his answer. "I read the dictionary!" he said. I thought that was a pretty boring summer, but it must have done him some good! Roy Lilly was elected class president during our sophomore, junior and senior years. He went on to become a Professor at Kent State. But he always chided me about losing the election our freshman year because of sympathy votes.

High school years flew by. I continued to work at the Crystal Theater as popcorn girl. Mom and Dad kept the business growing by bringing in the best movies. My brother Dan joined us when he was ten. He took over Dad's job as ticket-taker, leaving Dad to manage the business. Eventually, Dan worked in the projector room upstairs with Roger Coonley. He learned how to load rolls of film into the big machines and time the start of each reel, so the movie played without interruption.

One of Dad's jobs was 'behavior enforcer.' Often parents would drop their children off at the theater, leaving them unsupervised for a couple of hours. Any rowdy behavior was quickly squelched by my dad. He didn't tolerate loudness or running in the theater, and the kids knew he meant business. If he came down the aisle toward them, they quickly knew to hush up and settle down. Otherwise, they would be hauled out of the theater and their parents called. So, Dad earned a healthy respect, based somewhat on fear, but that was okay with him. He did not want decent paying customers disturbed during the movie by out-of-control children.

* * * * *

Being a teenager, it wasn't long before I began to be interested in boys. For some reason, I seemed to be most interested in guys who were older than me. When I was a sophomore in high school, I grabbed the eye of Bill Cleveland. He was five years older than me and had a motorcycle. I was mostly interested in the motorcycle, I must admit, but his flirting was fun, too!

Every day I walked home from school. It was over a mile, but I didn't mind. Sometimes I walked part way with friends, but the last little bit of my journey I was usually alone. As I got close to home, I cut down the alley behind Slater's Furniture Store. Then I passed by Fall's Products, a place that made lawn mowers. The windows of Fall's Products looked out over our back yard, where we had a fence covered with grape vines. When the grapes were ripe, I would stop and pick some to eat on the short walk to our back door.

Bill Cleveland worked at Fall's Products. He would watch for me from the windows of Fall's Products and when he saw me picking grapes, he always called down to me. "How about throwing me some of those grapes?"

One day I was walking uptown, and Bill rode by on his motorcycle. He pulled over and stopped beside me. "Hey, Kay, want a ride?" he asked. I had always wanted to ride on a motorcycle, so I eagerly agreed. We rode around town awhile and then he took me home. My mom was surprised to see me riding on the back of Bill's motorcycle.

Mom said, "Kay, you know he's a lot older than you. Your dad and I have always liked Bill; he's a friendly and good man. So, we don't mind you being with him, but please tell him to be careful. Tell him he needs to go slow with you on the motorcycle."

The flirting with Bill Cleveland came to an abrupt halt, however, when Fall's Products burst out in flames in the middle of the night. It was my junior year of high school. I was sound asleep when suddenly my mom was yelling "Get up everybody! There's a fire! Fire! Get up!"

As I opened my eyes, I glanced at the clock and saw it was about four in the morning. I smelled smoke but wasn't fully aware of what was going on. Mom hurried into my room and shook me to be sure I was awake, "Hurry! Get dressed. Fall's Products is on fire."

I dressed as fast as I could, but before I left my bedroom, I reached under my mattress and grabbed an envelope where I had stashed my hard-earned cash. The house might burn down, but I was going to save my money!

When I ran outside, I saw Dad and Dan on the roof of our house. They were using garden hoses to douse the roof so the fire wouldn't spread to us. I also saw men running in and out of Fall's

Products trying to save as many lawn mowers as they could. Soon the fire truck arrived and took over. A fire like this was attracting a lot of neighbors. It was big news.

While Dad was up on the roof with a garden hose, our neighbor, Helen Campbell, jumped into action. She ordered all the people standing around watching the fire to go into our house and bring the furniture out. She thought she was helping to save our furniture from the flames. As our sofa, chairs, lamps and tables were carted out the front door and carried across the street to safety, Dad came in from the backyard. He walked through the back door and into the bare living room.

"Where's all the furniture?" he shouted.

Helen Campbell was quick to explain. "We're taking it across the street, so it doesn't burn up!"

"What in the world, Helen?" Dad threw up his hands in disbelief. "We've got insurance, and that furniture is very old. Let it burn!"

The fire at Fall's Products was extinguished and things calmed down a little. Bystanders started to drift home. That's when I noticed tall, handsome Speedy (Floyd) Oursler standing off to the side. He was our new neighbor who had just moved with his grandma into the green house on the corner.

Our house was spared the flames and Dad insisted that our furniture be carried back inside. I picked up a lamp and headed to the front door. But I kept my eyes on the handsome man. When I came back out to get something else to carry in, I noticed that he was walking up Sycamore Street. I picked up a kitchen chair and slowly walked toward my house. I watched as he crossed the alley and went into the green house.

CHAPTER TWO
The Boy Next Door

Across the alley, on the corner and right near the theater, was the green house. Zula Rousch had lived there all my life, but now she was gone. In 1957, when I was a junior in high school, Grandma Hill moved into the green house. She used a wheelchair because she had lost the use of her legs. Even though she was handicapped, she was very independent. She could cook and clean and do other household chores. The only thing she couldn't do was walk. Using her feet to move the wheelchair, Grandma Hill would make her way down the ramp at her back door and take her laundry to the Laundromat, which was located on the other side of the theater.

Grandma Hill's grandson, Floyd, had lived with her since he was five years old. His mother had died, and his father sent him to live with Grandma Hill. Even though Floyd's dad had promised that he would come and get Floyd as soon as he was settled, he never did.

Floyd's dad would take him fishing for two weeks every summer. That was really the only contact he had with his dad. Floyd was never asked if he liked fishing, or if he wanted to do something else. It was just expected that for two weeks in the summer, they would be together and fish. So, Floyd suffered through several fishing trips, hating every minute of it. But his dad didn't notice, or care to ask. Eventually, Floyd found other things to do in the summer, so he didn't have to go fishing with his dad. They drifted even further apart. As Floyd got older, feelings of abandonment and resentment settled upon him.

Grandma Hill and Floyd lived across town while he was in elementary school. It wasn't until he was in high school that I even knew about him. By that time, he was tall and athletic and had earned the nickname of 'Speedy' because he had some fast moves on the basketball court.

When they moved into the green house, Speedy was already out of high school. I knew who he was (everyone knew the basketball stars) but he never acted like he even knew I was his neighbor. We didn't really have any reason to associate together because he was so much older than me.

All I knew of him was that he had been injured playing basketball. He had surgery on his knee while he was in high school. After that I heard that he went into the Marines. I didn't give him a second thought, until Grandma Hill moved next door and Speedy was suddenly my neighbor.

Speedy was twenty-one when he returned from a short time in the Marines. I learned that his basketball injury had become worse while he was with the Marines, and he needed more surgery. The Marines told him he could have the surgery done while still enlisted or he could return home to have it done there. Speedy chose to return home. Therefore, they gave him an honorable discharge for medical reasons, and he moved back to Grandma Hill's house.

When people would ask Speedy why he got out of the Marines so quickly, he would reply, "I ended the Korean War!" In truth, the Korean War had just ended, so it was a sensible time to be discharged.

I was sixteen. Speedy was definitely the best-looking eligible bachelor in town, and now he lived right next door to me!

I was quite smitten by this good-looking guy! I soon discovered that from my second story bedroom window I could look with binoculars and see right into Grandma Hill's kitchen. I spent many late evenings watching Grandma as she waited up for Speedy. And when he finally did come home, I could barely take my eyes off him. I sat at my window, spy glasses at the ready, watching his every move.

I quickly realized that Speedy was often drunk when he got home. I recognized all the behaviors because I could remember seeing my dad act the same way. I was eight when Dad stopped drinking, but I could remember what it was like before he finally quit. Stumbling, bumping into doorways, falling asleep instantly in his chair – I'd seen it all before.

Often Speedy would be helped into the house by his drinking buddy, his old basketball coach, Harry Henigan. Sometimes he was so drunk he couldn't make it up the stairs to the kitchen door without help. But that didn't really matter to me. Speedy was still the man of my dreams.

Before long, Speedy started to notice me, too. How could he not? I walked past his house every evening on my way to the theater. Eventually I worked up the nerve to talk to him. I offered to give him free popcorn when he came to the theater. I guess I changed my mind about using popcorn as bribery! But it worked. Pretty soon Speedy and I became a little more than friends. Before long I was getting him into the movies for free.

Speedy's basketball injury required several surgeries, and the recovery took time. He couldn't work and sold his car, so he'd have some money.

I didn't realize at the time, but Speedy was struggling. He was dealing with feelings of abandonment because of his dad. He was down and out because of his painful knee injury and ultimate discharge from the Marines. He used alcohol to dull the sense of uselessness. When he was drinking, he could forget his troubles. Speedy felt better about himself when he was hanging out at the local tavern with his former coach. They talked about Floyd's glory days on the basketball team in high school. The team had gone to state one year, and Speedy had been a star. That's how he got the nickname Speedy – because no one could keep up with him on the basketball court. Reminiscing on the good old days was a conversation that could raise his self-esteem.

As I learned more about Speedy and observed his drunken behaviors, my school-girl infatuation didn't disappear. In fact, my thinking was, 'All he needs is a good woman to straighten him out.' I imagined that I was just the woman he needed!

We started actually dating in my senior year. Since he didn't have a car, I asked Dad if Speedy could use his old Cadillac when we went on dates. Sometimes we went to the movie theater in Sycamore. I felt like a traitor, attending a theater that was in competition with my dad's. But Speedy would say, "We want to see that Kathryn Hepburn show, right? I know you love her movies. It hasn't come to the Crystal yet, so let's just go to Sycamore!" I did love Kathryn Hepburn, so we went!

We went dancing at the Blue Moon and went to lots of parties. There was always alcohol involved. I wasn't used to drinking because ever since Dad quit, there had never been alcohol in our house. I was still in high school, so I did not drink at these parties. Sometimes we double dated with my best friend, Donna, and her boyfriend, Rex.

One day I asked Speedy an important question. It took all the nerve I could muster to ask, "Would you go with me to my Senior Prom?"

Speedy had a quick answer. "Well, since I never got to go to my own prom because I was down with knee surgery, well, sure, I'll go to yours!"

CHAPTER THREE

Forming a Family

When I graduated from high school in the spring of 1958, Speedy and I were already an item. I was debating where I wanted to go for college and made my decision primarily on the proximity of the school to Speedy. I didn't want to be too far away from him, but I also didn't want to be so close that spending time together would interfere with my studies. I was determined to get good grades, wherever I went, and didn't want any distractions.

Speedy would be taking classes at Northern Illinois University, in DeKalb, which was only a twelve-mile drive from Genoa. He would continue to live with Grandma Hill and commute to classes.

I decided to attend the Northwest Institute of Medical Technology in Minneapolis. It was close enough that Speedy could visit me, and I could go home at Christmas. I shared an apartment with three other girls, Diane, Carol and Joyce. We each took turns cooking and cleaning. It was a good arrangement.

There was just one thing wrong. I was homesick! I missed my parents and even my brother. Sometimes, eating supper with my roommates, I would just burst into tears. My roommates were shocked but sympathetic. Gradually, after about six months, my fits of loneliness dissipated, and I could get back to full concentration on my studies.

The classes were intense, and I studied hard. We were learning about chemicals and laboratory tests on blood, urine and other bodily secretions. I also learned how to take and develop x-rays. There were lectures and lab experiences and so much to remember.

My roommates and I worked at St. Mary's Hospital on weekends. I was assigned to the maternity ward as an aide. I took temperatures, brought in food trays, and gave water to the new mothers. I was not allowed contact with the babies, but, oh boy, did I love looking at them through the nursery windows.

One day I asked Sister Margaret, the head nun, if I could *please* observe a birth. "I'm going to be married someday," I said, "And I would really like to see what having a baby is like." I think Sister Margaret liked me, because she agreed. She helped me dress like a student nurse and let me go into the delivery room with the students who were there that day. I was only supposed to observe, but one of the doctors assumed I was a student nurse, and he asked me to adjust the lighting. I did it, even though I was not really supposed to.

This young unmarried girl was going to give her baby up for adoption. In such a case, the birth mother was not allowed to see the baby. A sheet was placed over the patient's abdomen and knees, so she couldn't watch, and the newborn was quickly whisked away. The thinking at the time was that if the mother saw the baby, she would have second thoughts about giving the child up for adoption. I understood the reasoning, but it made me sad.

My schooling was going well. Speedy came to visit me a couple of times. I would pack a picnic lunch, and we would take a walk along the Mississippi River. Sitting on the riverbank sharing our lunch, he would fill me in on what was happening in Genoa. It was a little taste of home, and I looked forward to his visits.

When I went home for Christmas break, Speedy proposed. I happily accepted and we started making plans. We set the date for September 26, 1959. It would be two days after I graduated from medical laboratory school.

Neither of us wanted a big wedding, so we decided to get married in Minneapolis and invite whoever could come. My parents and brother, Dan, were there, and Speedy's Grandma Hill. A few of his aunts and uncles came, as did my roommates and close friends from Genoa. Some of Speedy's buddies came, too.

The night before the wedding, we had a rehearsal dinner at a nice club that had a DJ spinning records. When he learned that Speedy and I were about to be married, the DJ announced that he was playing a special song for us to dance to. But Speedy refused to dance with me, and I was surprised and hurt. We sat there as the music started playing, then other people got up to dance. My dad leaned over to me and whispered, "Kay, it's not too late to change your mind."

We were married the next day. We spent the first night of our honeymoon at a motel just across the river in Wisconsin. We were on our way to a fishing lodge on the Flambeau Flowage near Mercer, Wisconsin. That was an odd choice, since Speedy really did not like fishing. But he knew I did, so that's why he chose it. We didn't plan to do much fishing, anyway.

The first night we were together, we didn't get much sleep, for many reasons. One you may suspect, but there were more. As new couples arrived at the motel, their car lights shone right into our room. Every time the room lit up, we were disturbed. Neither Speedy nor I were used to sleeping in a bed with another person, so that was difficult for us. Finally, Speedy asked me if I would mind if he slept in the other bed. I agreed, and we both slept better after that.

I'm happy to report that we were quickly able to adapt to sleeping together and came to enjoy it very much. In fact, through the years to come, we learned to find comfort through the hard times by turning to each other. You might say sex was the glue that held us together when circumstances seemed to be pulling us apart.

We started our married life in a small apartment in Genoa. I had been recruited by a pathologist, Dr. DeGraffenreid. while I was still in Med Lab school, to come and work for him in Sycamore, Illinois. He operated a lab that worked with three hospitals in the area. I worked primarily at Sycamore Municipal Hospital. It was a full-time job Monday-Friday, and I was on-call evenings two weekends a month.

I liked the work – but I did not like being on-call. Here I was, newly wed, and being called away from my husband at odd hours of the night. When I had to go in to run some lab work on the weekend, I was the only one working and it was lonely. Often, I would have to drive twelve miles to the DeKalb hospital, draw the blood, go to the lab to run the tests, then return to the hospital with the results. The building was dark and cold and sometimes I felt uneasy, working alone in the lab. I also felt the weight of my job resting on my shoulders. Cross matching of blood for transfusions required careful attention. Depending on what my tests found, I would take pints of blood back to the hospital for use during a procedure if it was necessary. Sometimes the outcome of my lab work would determine the treatment for a patient. I wanted to be thorough with my findings – I didn't want to make a mistake that might result in a serious, maybe even life threatening, condition.

After I had worked there about six months, Dr. Ovitz asked me how I liked my job. I told him I liked the work but not the on-call weekends. He offered me a full-time job, with no on-call required. I'd be working at a clinic for three doctors: Dr. Ovitz, Dr. Thomas and Dr. Lindeen. The Elm Street Clinic in Sycamore had its own laboratory and was my workplace for the next three years. The doctors liked that I could do hematology, bacteriology and some chemistry lab work, as well as take x-rays and develop them. I liked the x-ray work. After developing the films, I was the first person to spot the broken arm or discover that the lady was going to have twins.

Speedy and I moved to Sycamore and lived in the upstairs apartment of Mrs. Kocker's home. Speedy was commuting to Genoa to work at Automatic Electric.

I left the Elm Street Clinic to stay home with my first child, Jill, who was born when I was twenty-two, and then Jon, who came along two years later. I devoted myself to housework and childcare. We moved back to Genoa just before Jon was born and bought our first house.

CHAPTER FOUR
Trouble in Paradise

Old habits are hard to kill, and Speedy kept going out with Coach Henigan and his friends. He was particularly wild on the weekends. Although he didn't drink at home, he was often difficult to live with. Speedy was never physically abusive to me when he was drinking. But we did have some pretty heated arguments about money.

Speedy was a spender, and I was a saver. I didn't like that he spent a lot of money on alcohol when I wanted to save for the future. He didn't like that I was so frugal and tried to keep him from just having fun. In the early years, nearly all of our arguments were about how to spend our money. One time Speedy yelled at me and said, "You're never satisfied, Kay. You'll never be happy until you have a thousand dollars in the bank!"

One of Speedy's friends, Jim Blankenbaker, had moved to Minnesota and was a Vice President at 3M company. He returned to Genoa for a visit with his parents and stopped by to see Speedy. In the course of conversation, Jim suggested that Speedy apply for a job with 3M. Jim knew of an opening in sales and would put in a good word for him. Speedy applied and was hired as a traveling salesman, which was great. But we had to move to North Carolina, and I was not excited about that. I didn't even know where North Carolina was!

"We can't move!" I said, trying to convince him to decline the position. "Mom's going through menopause, and I need to be here for her. And her eyesight is failing, and she needs me. Besides, the kids need their grandparents." I had a hundred and one excuses.

Speedy took me by the shoulders and made me look eye-to-eye with him. "You are my wife, Kay, and you *will* go where I tell you to go." He went on, "We'll buy a house. You'll make friends."

We moved to Greensboro, North Carolina, in 1965. I convinced Speedy that if he was going to have an important job with 3M, he needed to have a name that was more compatible with the position. A nickname like Speedy seemed out of place with a respectable job. From that point on, Speedy was known by his given name, Floyd.

Because Floyd's job was in sales, he traveled Monday through Friday and came home on weekends. That left me at home alone raising two small children.

While Floyd was traveling and working in North Carolina, he was also enjoying himself and living an easy life. He had an expense account and could entertain potential clients, which usually included fine dining and drinks. I'm sure he found life at home on the weekends to be pretty dull after his many business contacts. And truthfully, I sometimes preferred my quiet days with the children, when I didn't have to deal with Floyd's obnoxious behavior. I was finding out that, even though I was trying hard to be the good woman who could settle Floyd down and help him leave his drinking behaviors behind, it just wasn't going to be that easy. Floyd didn't see the problem alcohol was causing. Or maybe he just didn't want to recognize it.

Our next-door neighbors, Richard and Barbara, became good friends. But something about Richard puzzled Floyd, and one night he finally asked him about it. "Richard, I've been wondering something," he said. "Every night you leave the house after dinner, and you come home two hours later. What's up with that? Where do you go every night?"

Richard hesitated just a second and admitted, "I go to Alcoholics Anonymous meetings every night. I'm an alcoholic and the meetings help keep me sober."

Floyd just shook his head and said, "Good for you."

After two and a half years, Floyd was transferred to Towson, Maryland, and we moved again. Floyd's sales territory covered Maryland and Virginia. Once again, he usually traveled Monday-Friday and came home on weekends. He continued to drink and socialize while he was away on sales calls, and usually came home in a depressed, remorseful mood. He knew that his behavior Monday through Friday was not conducive to the family life he desired.

Floyd didn't drink when he was home on weekends, but he was often difficult to deal with. One time we had an argument, and I went into our bedroom and locked the door. Floyd was furious that I had locked him out. He broke the door down! He rushed into the bedroom, shaking his finger at me and yelling "Don't you ever do that again!" His face was red with anger, and I knew he was really upset, but he didn't physically hurt me.

CHAPTER FIVE

A Wake-Up Call

Drinking continued to be a normal part of Floyd's life. He drank to be social, to entertain clients and to avoid the problems that he didn't want to deal with. Sometimes he just drank to pass the time. One night, after a sales meeting in Virginia, Floyd stumbled to his hotel room and passed out.

When he awoke the next day, he was confused. He lay on his hotel bed, fully dressed in his suit and even his shoes. His hands were folded over his chest as if he were lying in a casket. At first, he thought he was already dead. It gave him quite a scare. That was a turning point in Floyd's life. He finally realized what his drinking had done to him, and he knew he needed help before it killed him.

Addictions are so powerful. If you are not personally involved with someone with an addiction, it's easy to judge them and say, 'Just quit.' But an addiction can have such a hold on a person that they don't see rationally. When they finally realize they need help, the addict has a struggle ahead. Staying clean is very difficult. Floyd knew he wasn't strong enough to do it on his own. He knew he needed help.

He called our old neighbor, Richard, in North Carolina. "Richard," he said. "I think I have a drinking problem."

"I think you do, too," was Richard's answer. He gave Floyd some information about Alcoholics Anonymous, and Floyd contacted them when he got home.

A man from AA came to visit with us. He was doing what was called in AA as a Twelve Step Call, and Floyd was his first contact. I wasn't impressed with him – he seemed shaky and barely sober himself. But Floyd really listened and from that point on, he went to AA meetings most evenings. He even sought out AA meetings while he was on the road and attended as often as he could. After that frightening event in a Virginia hotel room, Floyd never took another drink. He was thirty years old when he kicked that addiction, and he lived the next fifty-one years sober.

I joined an Al-Anon group and was a member for thirty-seven years. The meetings helped me support Floyd as he battled his addiction and also helped me learn how to cope with the changes his sobriety brought to our family. Floyd and I agreed that we wanted our marriage to be better and our family life more stable.

Besides our AA support groups, Floyd and I went to counseling together. We found family counseling and marriage counseling both to be helpful. Finally, our lives were coming together, and we were happy. The children loved their schools, and I felt like we were settling into the routines of a happy family. Floyd still traveled for work, but he came home on Fridays eager to be an involved father and spend time with his family.

One weekend, Floyd proposed that we start 'family night.' He thought that every Friday we should plan activities for the four of us to do together. It was a great idea – if only he had thought of it sooner. "It's too late," I told him. "The kids are so busy with school activities and other things with their friends."

Jill and Jon loved going roller skating every Friday night. The elementary school opened up its gym for skating. I knew the kids would not want to give up that activity. Despite that little setback, Floyd did what he could to be a good dad.

The Floyd Oursler Family - 1972

With all the support groups and counseling sessions we attended, things began to improve. That doesn't mean, however, that everything was sunshine and roses. Floyd wasn't drinking, but his attendance at nightly AA meetings meant that he was absent from the home a lot. That meant that most of the child-rearing and housekeeping and maintenance was left to me.

One day, the kitchen sink backed up and wouldn't drain. I asked Floyd to fix it, which he was totally capable of doing, but he was on his way out to work. He told me what tools I would need, what parts to pick up at the hardware store, and how to change the gooseneck, and then he left for work. I was angry that he put it all on me. I thought he should have stayed home and taken on the responsibility for the repair, instead of passing it off to me. Even so, I worked on that sink until it drained properly. It's amazing what one can do when one must.

CHAPTER SIX
A Seed is Planted

About this time, I was watching television, and a news report came on about the excellent work that was being done by the Peace Corps. Started by President Kennedy in 1961, the goal of Peace Corps was to teach and train people in remote parts of the world, while at the same time learning about their culture. The purpose was to promote world peace and friendship. I was amazed with what I learned about young, educated Americans sharing their knowledge and skills with under-developed countries around the world.

I told Floyd what I had learned and said I might be interested in joining Peace Corps someday, but his only response was, "That's a crazy idea."

True, this might not be the right time for me to consider such an adventure. Young children still in school, a household to manage, parents who needed me - there were many reasons to forget the whole idea. But maybe someday......

Unexpectedly, Floyd announced that he was being relocated – to Chicago. Although a move to Chicago would mean being closer to my family, I was not happy about the prospect. I was content in Towson. We had lots of good friends there and enjoyed socializing with them. I had a good part time job with a pathology lab and was taking classes from Towson State. Floyd was taking classes too, in psychology. It just didn't seem like a good time for a move, and I wasn't happy.

Jill and Jon didn't want to move either. They didn't want to leave their school and the friends they had made. In fact, Jill put up a real fuss and refused to move. She only agreed to it after her dad promised her a pony.

So, we packed up and moved to Palatine, Illinois, a suburb of Chicago. We were about fifty miles from Genoa, where Floyd and I grew up and still had family and friends. Unfortunately, we found that things were very expensive in the Chicago area, and we couldn't afford to get a pony for Jill. Needless to say, she was not happy about that.

Floyd settled into life in Chicago. He had become a staunch believer in the value of therapy and counseling and decided that he wanted to take more classes in psychology and family counseling. His goal was to get his bachelor's degree in psychology.

I had a job with Equitable Life working in the medical claims department. The office was just a mile from home, which made it ideal. I enjoyed the work and decided to take some classes on the weekend as well. Things were tight financially, but we were doing okay.

Once Floyd quit drinking, he developed another habit. I'm not sure how or why, but the pounds were creeping up on him. Instead of alcohol, Floyd turned to sugary foods for comfort and as an escape. Ice cream became his snack of choice. It was not unusual for him to eat a half gallon or more at one time. Before long, he had gained an unhealthy amount of weight. Being a believer in group therapy and counseling support groups, Floyd joined Overeaters Anonymous and took off about forty pounds. It was another area of his life he struggled with but was able to overcome. He felt good about that, and he looked pretty good, too.

Our marriage wasn't perfect; there were many issues we had to work through. An incident happened with Floyd at work, and we decided to seek marriage counseling. Addictions come in many forms and can have long-lasting consequences. But Floyd and I learned, through counseling and lots of prayer, to manage our disappointments and fears. We took the tough times along with the good, knowing that our marriage would be strong enough as long as we communicated and trusted each other.

CHAPTER SEVEN

Adventures in New York City

My job with Equitable Life was going well. I enjoyed the work and felt I was doing a good job. Those in management must have thought so, too, because one day I received a phone call from the branch manager in Des Moines, Iowa.

"Kay," he said, "There's a job opportunity coming up, and I have recommended you to attend. You'll be working on a new computer program for processing medical and dental claims. It's a great chance for learning and advancement with our company."

He went on to explain the details. They would send me to New York City for three to four weeks. I would have all expenses paid while there - hotel, food, travel, everything. The job sounded interesting, and I could see how it would help me in my work.

I felt flattered that he had thought of me when the job opened up. I didn't consider myself all that smart or capable, but apparently, he did. It was an honor to be selected for the position. "And once you've been at this job for awhile, you'll be on track for a promotion to manager," he added. It was an enticing offer, to be sure.

It seemed too good to be true. Maybe the Lord was orchestrating all this, because it certainly wasn't something I had initiated or even heard of. It came to me out of the blue and I was stunned.

But I immediately said 'No." How could I go away for a month? I needed to be home with my husband and son. And New York City! A big place like that, all on my own, no, I couldn't do that.

The very thought was overwhelming. So, I turned down the offer. I knew I passed up the opportunity of a lifetime, but I lacked the confidence to venture that far from home on my own.

When Floyd came home, I told him about the phone call. He was pleased that my work had been recognized and that I had been recommended for this amazing opportunity. And he didn't understand why I had turned it down. "You should go," he said. "Jon is in college; he's a grown man. He can take care of himself. He doesn't need you to babysit him anymore!"

"But it doesn't seem right, leaving you," I protested.

"Kay, if you don't take this opportunity, you'll never know what you've missed. I've taken classes and received my counseling degree. I'm working on my master's and will be focused on that for the whole time you're gone. The kids are grown and on their own. Jill has moved away; Jon is in college. It's your turn now. Call the guy back and tell him you changed your mind. Go. Take the job and learn all you can. It'll be good for you. Go."

So, I did.

* * * * *

There were six of us sent to New York to work on the new computer program. We were all from different Equitable offices throughout the United States. Dallas and I were put up at the Sheraton City Squire Hotel in midtown Manhattan. We traveled by bus or subway to Battery Park where we worked from seven in the morning until three in the afternoon, with a break for lunch. That left us with plenty of free time in the late afternoon and evenings.

Friends in New York City

There was so much to see and do! Instead of intimidating me, the Big Apple invigorated me. Somehow, I was appointed to the position of Social Director for the six of us girls. I was happy to plan outings for sight-seeing or dinners out. We saw thirteen plays on Broadway! Sometimes we just met for bagels and coffee. We visited the Brooklyn Zoo and Central Park. We traveled to Ellis Island on a Circle Line Cruise boat but couldn't tour the Statue of Liberty because it was under reconstruction. We went to the Empire State Building and the World Trade Center. It was a vacation-like atmosphere, with work thrown in on the side.

What was supposed to be three or four weeks of training stretched into six months. I was in New York City from January until June in1985. My expenses were still being paid, and it seemed I had unlimited company money. Equitable even paid for our travel to and from New York City, including vacation visits. They would pay for me to fly home or for Floyd to come to NYC to visit me every other weekend.

Floyd was taking classes to get his master's from Adler Institute, so he had a lot of studying to do. He did come to visit me a couple of times while I was there. I showed him around some of my favorite new places. I introduced him to my new friends. I enjoyed his visits, but I realized that I was not as homesick as I thought I might be. I remembered the long days and nights when I had been hospitalized with back surgery, and I recalled how lonely and homesick I had been. I remembered my homesickness for the first six months of school in Minneapolis. But it was different now. Being on my own in New York City had changed me. I felt more independent, adventurous and confident than I ever had before.

Every Friday evening, the Sheridan hosted 'VIP Night.' Dallas and I were always invited. There was an open bar with free cocktails and wine. There were delicious hors d'oeuvres of shrimp, crab and other delights, even caviar! We always looked forward to our Friday evenings where we could really let down and relax. We met people from all over the world.

It was a very exciting time in my life. I grew emotionally and socially and became a more confident woman. By the end of the six months in New York City, I was feeling like I could take on the world. I was promoted to a management position, overseeing more than sixty employees.

Marriage counseling, support groups and job satisfaction helped to build up my belief in myself. The roller-coaster of our marriage seemed to be slowing to a calmer, more level ride. Things were going well.

In 1987, at age 52, Floyd received his master's degree in marriage and family counseling from Adler Institute in Chicago. With his degree came a new job opportunity with 3M. He was now working as an employee counselor for 3M in a program called the Employee Assistance Program. He facilitated counseling sessions for employees going through a variety of personal and work-related issues. Floyd usually did one-on-one sessions. He also had a list of counselors located near 3M locations across the country so he could refer clients for outside help. He was good at his job and helped many people.

CHAPTER EIGHT

Revisiting an Old Idea

About this time, I read an article about the good work the Peace Corps was doing in underdeveloped countries around the world. The idea still intrigued me, and I sent away for some information. The children were grown and married, and it seemed like the time might be right for a new direction in my life. When the brochures arrived in the mail a few weeks later, I showed them to Floyd and said, "I think I might like to do this."

Just like the first time I showed an interest in Peace Corps, Floyd was strongly opposed to the concept. I wanted to talk it over calmly, but Floyd immediately shot the whole idea to pieces. "Why would somebody want to go halfway around the world, live with uncivilized natives, be exposed to all sorts of illnesses and dangers, and for what?"

"It could do a lot of good," I said. "It would be an adventure. And it might teach those 'uncivilized natives' ways to become more civilized. I think it's a great idea."

With a huff and a "Huh," Floyd ended the conversation. As far as Floyd was concerned, the subject was closed. But I kept the brochures and read them over cover to cover. The testimonials of some of the volunteers intrigued me. It seemed like the Peace Corps experience had changed both the 'uncivilized natives' and the volunteers themselves. It sounded like a wonderful program.

Floyd might not approve, but I couldn't dismiss the idea that quickly.

CHAPTER NINE
More Changes

My mom and dad were getting older and decided to retire to Florida to get away from the harsh Illinois winters. While there, Dad was diagnosed with lung cancer. He had been smoking since the age of ten, when he worked as a caddy at the West Chicago golf course. He had, however, quit smoking seven years prior to retirement, but the damage had already been done. Such a deadly habit had finally caught up with him. Maybe it should be called an addiction. Is there a Quit Smoking support group?

When it looked like Dad's time on earth was nearing an end, I took time off from my job with Equitable and went to Florida. I was in the hospital sitting with Dad one day when his doctor came in. I asked him what caused Dad to have cancer. The surgeon pulled a pack of cigarettes out of his own lab coat and said, "These right here." It seemed so ironic to me – that a doctor should have known better, but here he was, still smoking himself. Yes, I'd definitely call it an addiction.

After Dad passed, Mom stayed living in Bradenton, Florida. Her eyesight was failing, and I was worried about her. But she insisted she was fine. She had friends there and wanted to stay put.

* * * * *

When we moved to Palatine, Illinois, Floyd had expected that we would be relocated in a couple of years. That seemed to be the pattern we had fallen into. His sales territory changed often, which required frequent moves.

But after he received his master's degree in Marriage and Family Counseling from Adler Institute, his job description changed, and Floyd thought we would be relocated to the Twin City area of Minnesota, where the 3M home office was located. We ended up staying in Palatine for a total of eighteen years. Floyd would travel from Palatine to various 3M locations as needed. Eventually we were relocated to the Twin Cities.

Our next move was to Cottage Grove, Minnesota, a suburb of Saint Paul. We built our dream home, and it was perfect. We had a lovely backyard with room for relaxing and entertaining. When we were planning the house, we even included a mother-in-law suite for Mom because Floyd thought it would be best if she lived with us. Mom was still resistant, however, so we didn't push it. The rooms were ready for her, if and when she ever decided to move to Minnesota.

Mom did move in with us in 1993, shortly after we moved in ourselves. Her best friend in Florida had decided to get married, and Mom didn't want to be a third wheel. She was also beginning to realize she was going to need help. Her vision was declining rapidly and in her later years, she was completely blind.

We became active members of our church in Cottage Grove. The congregation was meeting in a school and getting ready to build a new church. One day the pastor came to me and asked if I would oversee the capital campaign. He knew of my experience with management and budgeting because of my work with Equitable Life. I was hesitant at first because I had never done fundraising, but I soon threw myself into the project. Our committee helped to raise enough money to cover all the initial costs. Once construction started, I organized teams of church members to do a lot of the work ourselves. I was so thankful that my dad had modeled a strong work ethic. Our team of volunteers applied the Tyvek wrap and put in the insulation. We learned how to use screw guns for the drywall we hung on the ceiling. We did most of the painting.

All this construction knowledge came in handy both in Cottage Grove and halfway around the world, years later. And little did I know at the time, but my fundraising experiences would also be helpful in my future. It seems like, all along my life, God had been preparing me for the next step. I didn't know it then, but I can see it now.

I was working part time for Aflac selling supplemental insurance. Early each afternoon, I would go home after work, check on Mom, then rush over to the church building site. I would talk with the general contractor, George, and find out what he needed our volunteers to do that evening. Usually our team worked from 6:00 – 10:00 in the evening.

It was a very busy and sometimes stressful time. George and I butted heads a few times. One day I was contacted by a man named Jim from Austin, Minnesota. Jim was a good man who believed in helping start-up churches. Every year he would give one week of his time to work on the construction of a new church. His expertise was in tiling, and the church needed tile work on the kitchen and bathroom floors and walls. Jim said he would come to Cottage Grove for a week and do all that work for free. We just had to house and feed him for the week. It was a great deal, and I was all for it.

George, the general contractor, was not so sure, however. He had already arranged to pay a team for that work. I held my ground, though, and said, "Why would we pay somebody to do the work when I can get it done for free?"

Not only did the church get the work done for free, but I learned another valuable skill -how to lay tile. In hindsight, I understand what a great blessing this knowledge would be to me, in a different place and time. It was another example of how God was preparing me for the work he had planned for me to do later.

Mom passed away on Feb. 1, 2002, six days before her 87th birthday. I was happy to be her caregiver to the very end. I recalled how she had selflessly and kindly cared for me those many years ago when I was recovering from spinal surgery. Now it was my turn to take care of her.

And I was thankful that Floyd had insisted that she live with us. It was definitely the best thing we could have done for Mom, and it was all because of Floyd's planning that we were able to do it. Although he chuckled and said, "But I didn't know she was going to be here nine years!"

With the money from the sale of Mom's villa in Florida, we purchased a townhouse in Hot Springs Village, Arkansas. We knew we liked the area because we had been there many times golfing with Floyd's co-workers from 3M. We bought the home as an investment and had renters living there for a couple of years.

CHAPTER TEN
A New Addiction

Floyd was in support groups for his addictions of drinking and overeating. After Floyd got control of his sugar addiction, he stopped going to Overeaters, but his devotion to AA meetings continued for the rest of his life. I was supported by attending Al-Anon meetings. We had been in family counseling, and our marriage counseling sessions continued. You might think that that was enough. With all we knew about therapy and support groups, with all we had learned about self-control and overcoming temptations, we should have been prepared for whatever troubling situations came our way, right? Wrong.

Floyd had always laughed about a saying that went around 3M. It was said that 3M stood for 'Many Many Meetings.' Now he was once again being sent off to meetings. 3M was holding an EAP conference in Las Vegas, and Floyd was attending. I was not prepared for how that one trip would affect the rest of our lives.

We had never been gamblers. We had gone to casinos once in a while just for fun, but it wasn't a usual activity for us. That was about to change, for Floyd anyway.

To get to the EAP conference rooms, attendees had to pass through the casino area of the hotel. Floyd found himself with some extra time before his meeting started, and he put a dollar into a slot machine. Out came $1,500.00, and Floyd was hooked. He told me the adrenaline rush was like nothing he had ever felt before. It was great when he was winning, but before long he realized that he had a problem. Gambling had become his latest addiction, and this was a very costly addiction, indeed.

Floyd knew he had a problem, and he knew he couldn't kick it without help. So, in true Floyd fashion, he joined a support group. Now he added Gambler's Anonymous to his list of meetings. It was different this time, though. He went to the meetings, he said the right things and acted the right way while he was there, but nothing had really changed. His gambling continued in secret. He was hiding his gambling behavior, and no one knew.

But Floyd knew, and it was making him miserable. For some reason, he just couldn't stop. He was falling deeper and deeper into debt, spending far more than he won. I was unaware of the devastation we were headed for. During our whole marriage, Floyd's paycheck went to cover the house payment, and my money paid for food. We also had been putting money into a savings account. It had worked fine that way, but it all changed at one o'clock one morning.

I was asleep but woke up when I heard Floyd crying. He stood in the bedroom doorway, eyes puffy and red, tears streaming down his cheeks.

I ran to him instantly, fearing he had bad news about one of the children. "What's wrong, Floyd? Are you okay? What happened?" He just kept crying.

Finally, I got him to calm down enough to explain. "I've lost all my money," he sobbed. "I don't have enough to make the house payment."

"Lost your money? What do you mean? Were you robbed?" I couldn't wrap my head around what he was saying.

"Gambling," he moaned. "I lost it all gambling."

"But I don't understand," I said. "You're going to Gambler's Anonymous. I thought you had quit gambling. I thought that was all over."

That's when Floyd slumped to the floor, totally defeated. "I've been going, but I've been lying to everybody. To them, to you, to everybody. I can't quit. It has such a hold on me. I just can't get past it. And now we don't have enough money to make the house payment, and it's all my fault."

I sat beside him and tried to console him. "I have money put away," I said. "I can cover the payment. But Floyd, you have to stop this. You have to."

He promised he would try harder. But gambling had a real hold on him. Ultimately, it led to the end of our marriage.

* * * * *

You've no doubt heard the saying 'kiss and make up.' It was certainly true in our marriage. Whenever we had a problem, whenever we were angry or hurt, whenever negative feelings were overwhelming, we turned to each other. Sex had kept our marriage together through all of our difficult times. We could find comfort and strength in each other's arms. We survived all the hard times because we had each other.

But now things were different. Floyd continued to gamble, continued to attend Gambler's Anonymous support groups, and continued to lie about his addiction. He was ashamed of himself and guilt-ridden. He shut down and withdrew. I was worried and didn't know what else I could do to help him.

One night I reached for Floyd as we lay in bed together. I wanted to 'kiss and make up.' I hoped intimacy would help him through his feelings of inadequacy. My heart was broken when Floyd turned away from me. Overcome with feelings of worthlessness, shame and guilt, he rolled over and faced the wall. I began to cry. We slept back-to-back that night, me with tears staining my pillow, Floyd with demons of defeat plaguing his dreams.

The next morning, Floyd announced, "I'm moving out. I'm just making your life miserable. I can't keep doing this to you. I'm just sick about this gambling. It's a terrible addiction and I can't quit. I go to the meetings, but I just tell one lie after another. You deserve better."

Floyd called our friend Gary and asked if he could stay at his house for awhile. We had known Gary and his wife, Joan, the whole time we had lived in Cottage Grove. Gary was our financial adviser as well as a good friend.

Gary and Joan were at the movies at the time of Floyd's call, but Gary told him where the spare key was and how to get into the house. With my help, Floyd packed a few belongings and went to stay with them.

Floyd moved into an apartment in 2003. I was still living in our dream home, but now it was empty and lonely. We had lived there for twelve years, and the house had always been bustling with activity. We did a lot of entertaining in those twelve years. Now the house was too big and too quiet.

I was alone. All my friends were also Floyd's friends, and I felt uncomfortable no longer being a part of a couple. I felt like Floyd's addiction had not only ruined his life, but it had also ruined mine.

We agreed to sell our beautiful house and split the profits. Gary, being our financial adviser, was tasked with the job of helping us divide assets equally. I know that was difficult for him. As our friend, he tried so hard to be fair to each of us.

CHAPTER ELEVEN

The Volunteer Spirit

After we sold our dream home, I went to live with my friend, Judy Anderson, in Hastings, Minnesota. Her husband had recently passed away, and we were both suddenly alone. Being together was a good situation for both of us. I kept busy with Aflac work and volunteered in a nursing home. I enjoyed getting to know the residents. Every day at 5:00, they had happy hour, and I was the bartender! I had strict instructions – each resident was allowed only one drink. One evening a resident asked for a second. I told him I had already given him one drink, and I wasn't supposed to serve more. If I did, I'd get fired. He laughed and said, "They can't fire you! You're a volunteer!"

While I volunteered at the nursing home, I was able to use their fitness center. So, I exercised there several times a week. I kept as physically active as I could and kept my mind busy as well. I was searching for a purpose in my life. I knew I still had a lot to give, even though I no longer had children or a husband or even an ailing parent to care for. Maybe, for the first time in my life, I was completely free to go wherever I wanted and do as I pleased.

I decided to renew my interest in the Peace Corps. Yes, I knew that most people joined the Peace Corps in their twenties, and here I was, over sixty. But I was healthy, fit, and eager to do some good in the world. I figured, "It's now or never!"

* * * * *

Thus began one of the biggest adventures of my lifetime.

PART THREE

BECOMING BIBI KAY

Peace Corps - A Little History

The Peace Corps has been an official organization of the United States since March 1, 1961, when President John F. Kennedy signed an executive order for its formation. The program was authorized by Congress in September of that year. The mission of the Peace Corps is to train and deploy volunteers to provide international development assistance. Sargent Schriver was the first director of the organization and served until 1966.

In the first year of its existence, the Peace Corps had 900 volunteers who served in sixteen countries. Six years later, the volunteers numbered 14,500 and were placed in fifty-five countries. Today there are currently over 2,400 volunteers working alongside community members in fifty-eight countries.

The stated mission of the Peace Corps is to promote world peace and friendship by fulfilling these goals:
1. Help countries interested in meeting their need for trained people
2. Help promote better understanding of Americans on the part of the people served
3. Help promote a better understanding of other peoples on the part of Americans

Volunteers undergo two to three months of in-country training where they learn to respect local customs, learn the prevailing language and live in comparable conditions. They are instructed on matters of health, safety and security as well as cultural norms.

Volunteers live and work alongside the people they serve. They collaborate with local governments, schools, small businesses and entrepreneurs to create sustainable community-based projects that address local development priorities.

Volunteers are encouraged to assist the communities with education, health, agriculture, entrepreneurship, women's empowerment and community development. Each volunteer serves for two years, although it's possible to extend an extra year. The average age for volunteers is twenty-six. Women make up 65% of the workforce, Couples are allowed to serve together but make up only 1% of the group.

Transportation costs are covered by the Peace Corps to and from the country where the volunteers serve. They are paid a wage that should provide them with a sustainable lifestyle and be able to support them well while serving in their assigned locations.

Living and working side by side with community members, Peace Corps volunteers build relationships, exchange cultures and knowledge and help transform lives for generations. Testimonials of retired Peace Corps Volunteers emphasize that their own lives have been transformed as completely as the lives of the community members they served.

CHAPTER ONE
Waiting

I was sixty-four years old. My children were grown, my husband was gone. At this point in my life, I was retired, single and free. My home was sold, and I had nothing to tie me down. My thinking was, 'If I don't do it now, I never will.'

While I was working, raising my family and running my home, my interest in Peace Corps and the desire to do some good in the world had been temporarily set aside. With my new-found freedom, thoughts of Peace Corps returned.

In 2003, while I was living with Judy Anderson in Hastings, Minnesota, I met with a Peace Corps recruiter. I filled out an application and waited and waited. Every few months I would call the headquarters in Washington, D.C. to check on the status of my paperwork.

In 2004, I moved to my townhouse in Hot Springs Village, Arkansas. Floyd and our son, Jon, helped me move my things down from Minnesota. As soon as I got settled, I updated my contact information with the Peace Corps. And I waited some more.

I didn't know many people in Hot Springs Village, so I started looking for something to do and a chance to meet people. I took the community newspaper, *The Voice,* and read about some activities that interested me. I decided to try out a hiking group that was meeting the next weekend. There I met Michael Moriarty and his little dog, Suzie. Michael was the leader of the hiking group and Suzie accompanied him on many of the hikes.

I learned that Michael lived in my neighborhood and his wife had recently passed away. He was a friendly man and welcomed me to the hiking group. After our first hike, Michael said to me, "Just let me know if you need anything. I'm pretty handy and can come over to your house to help you with whatever." I appreciated his kindness.

A couple of weeks later, I took him up on his offer. I was trying to clean my kitchen soffits, up on a ladder, holding a canister vacuum cleaner. I realized how dangerous it was and decided to call Michael for help. He came right over, steadied the ladder and held the canister while I cleaned. When we were finished, I walked him to the door and thanked him for the help. He had gotten halfway across the street when I opened the door and called him to come back.

"I'm not looking for a husband, but I do get lonely," I said to Michael. "It would be nice to have a companion, so I don't do everything alone; maybe play Scrabble or go out to dinner. Just for companionship, you know."

Michael's response was quick. "How about dinner Friday night?" From that point on, our friendship grew into more than just companionship. We even pooled our money and bought a motor home. The rest of 2004 was filled with hiking and biking. We traveled through the west, seeing sights in Colorado and Montana and hiking up the 14,000-foot mountains there.

Michael sometimes laughed about all the women who brought him casseroles after his wife passed away. He figured they had more on their minds than just providing him with nutrition. They probably wanted to start up a relationship with him. "But not Kay!" he'd say. "Kay gave me her vacuum and put me to work!"

Michael was a very thoughtful man, and we had many wonderful experiences together. He always put me first, always wanted what was best for me and always considered my needs.

Finally in December of 2004, I got the news I had been hoping for. I received an invitation to join the Peace Corps. On June 15, 2005, I was to fly to the east coast to meet with the group of volunteers headed for Tanzania, Africa, and start my life-changing adventure.

I asked Michael's opinion. We talked about the opportunity and how it would change things between us. I asked him if he wanted me to go.

Michael took my hands in his and said, "Hell, no! But if you don't go now, you may always regret it. I would never tell you to stay here; I wouldn't want you to hold it against me. Go and fulfill your dream."

CHAPTER TWO
And So It Begins
June 15, 2005

There were thirty-three of us in my training group. Most of the other volunteers were much younger than me, just out of college. Some of them had joined Peace Corps for the adventure of seeing the world. Some had joined because they couldn't get jobs in their major. Some just wanted to get away from home. And many of us were hoping to really make a difference in the world.

We were divided into three groups; my group was the environmentalists (laughingly referred to as the 'mentals'). There were fourteen Peace Corps Volunteers (PCVs) in the environmental group. The other two groups were health and education trainees, of which there were nineteen. Before the end of our training period, five of the volunteers returned to the United States for personal or medical reasons. One had malaria, some were lonely for their boyfriends, others had personal reasons

We flew from the United States to Amsterdam to Dar es Salaam, Tanzania. Let me tell you a little bit about Dar es Salaam. It is a city of about six million people and is the seaport capital for trade in Tanzania. Throughout the year, it is hot and humid with an average temperature of 29 Celsius (84 Fahrenheit). June, July and August are considered winter months, but it is still hot. October through April is the hottest time, with little or no rain. Being on the coast of the Indian Ocean, it is a bustling, somewhat modern city. There are many embassies and elegant hotels. But as with many large cities, there are also pockets of poverty. Overcrowding and congestion have been a few of the problems there. Dar es Salaam was the capital of Tanzania until 1996. At that time, the political capital was moved to Dodoma, which is more centrally located. Dar es Salaam continues to be the economic and trade capital of the country.

When we arrived, it was winter. Yet the temperature was too hot for me. I had specifically asked Peace Corps not to send me to a hot climate. I was assured that the village where I was being placed was in the mountains and thus cooler than the city seaport. I was thankful for that.

During training, I lived with my host family in Dar. (We quickly shortened the name of the city.) John was a successful farmer, and his wife, Elaina, was a nurse. They knew some English and were a big help to me learning Swahili.

They had several children, and I quickly got attached to their little girl who was about eight or nine years old. I soon noticed that parents in Tanzania didn't show affection to their children. There wasn't a lot of holding or hugging or any physical touch. When I asked Elaina about it, she told me, "We show our love with extra meat at dinner." I immediately recognized that as a big difference in cultures, and I soon realized how true that statement really was. Meat was seldom available for meals. Protein was lacking in most diets.

I was soon given the title 'Bibi Kay.' Bibi is a Tanzanian term used to show respect for an older woman. It often applies to grandmothers or other wise women. I was honored to have that nickname.

I was fortunate, because John and Elaina's home had electricity and a freezer. Most of the other volunteers were not so lucky. We had to bring our own drinking water to class, and one day all the water at my host home was frozen. So, I was late getting to class because I had to wait for some of the water to thaw so I could put it into my canteen. Some of the other volunteers booed me and laughed at the 'hardship' of having to wait for water to thaw.

Another big cultural difference I learned right away was impressed upon us in training. The instructor said, "Learn how to bathe with a cup of water." I discovered that to be true because water had to be carried from the village faucet or from the nearby rivers. One of the volunteers, Renee, paid a child shillings (a nickel) to go get her water from the river. We certainly didn't want to waste the water, so we learned to be careful with our water usage.

We were also told to be aware of mosquitoes. We were instructed to always wear long pants and long sleeves because we surely didn't want to be bitten by a disease-laden insect. I was fortunate, I guess, because mosquitoes didn't seem to like me. Malaria was certainly a possibility. Many of the volunteers took doxycycline daily as a prophylaxis, just in case. I took a Mefloquine pill once a week until I learned that there was a connection between Mefloquine and liver damage. Since my liver had been compromised because of my blood transfusions during spinal surgery, I didn't want to risk more complications. In the 1980's I had donated blood for the Red Cross. That's when I learned that I was a hepatitis C carrier and would never be allowed to donate blood again. So, because my liver was compromised, I didn't want to do anything that might cause further damage. Many volunteers tried Mefloquine, but the side effects were hallucinations and nightmares, so they soon decided to take doxycycline instead.

There was one other trainee who was about the same age as me. His name was Ed, and we became friends, partly because of our shared history. Unfortunately, Ed tore his Achilles tendon during training and was sent back to the United States. I learned later that he had returned to Tanzania after he had recovered from the surgery, only to be sent state-side again when he contracted TB. He told me "I guess I just wasn't meant to be in the Peace Corps."

Our two months of training were intense, especially the language part. Most of the younger volunteers picked up the language quickly, but I struggled. Before we 'passed' our training and were sent out to the villages, we had to take a language test. We would be interviewed one by one, in Swahili. I knew I would have no trouble with the written part of the test, but the interview section had me worried. I wrote out my biography in Swahili and memorized it. When it came time for the test, I launched into my 'speech.' Afterwards, I asked the teacher if I had passed. She said that yes, I had, but "You didn't even give me a chance to ask you any questions in Swahili!" I breathed a sigh of relief!

Our graduation ceremony was held, and we had a great time celebrating afterwards. We hosted a party for our host families and each of the volunteers provided entertainment. We put on a variety show of talent. I played my flutophone that I had learned to play in fifth grade. I was glad I had brought it along! One of the volunteers, Chris Brown, did a hilarious dance with crepe paper streamers and we all laughed so hard. It was a wonderful time of companionship and joy.

As the party came to a close, I walked out to the terrace with Shawn Block, another volunteer, and one of our teachers. Shawn looked at me and said, "Well, we made it!"

We congratulated each other and together started a little chant. "Look at me, I'm a PCV." We repeated it over and over as we walked arm in arm back into the party. Soon the other volunteers picked up the chant. Indeed, we all could say, "We made it!"

CHAPTER THREE
Getting Settled

My village, Uhekule, is near the Kipengere Mountain Range in the southern highlands and has an elevation of about 6000 feet. The trip from Dar es Salaam to Uhekule was quite an adventure. We traveled in a Peace Corps van that was driven by a Peace Corps driver. The road, if you could call it that, was rough and filled with deep potholes. We couldn't make the trip in one day, so we had to stay overnight in Njombe. The next day, as we drove closer and closer to Uhekule, my excitement rose. But I must admit, I was a bit apprehensive as well. This was a whole new world, and I was obviously out of place. As the only white person in the village, and an older person at that, I wondered how I would be received.

My traveling companion was a local Peace Corp trainer named Mwasha. He spoke good English and told me, "Don't worry. I know how to handle villagers." I was thankful for his reassurance. It was the first of many times that he gave me confidence.

Driving down a dusty road towards Uhekule village, we passed women working in the *viazi* (potato) fields. Some had babies strapped to their backs. They carried a *jembe* (large heavy hoe.) The women were cultivating their *shamba* (fields) with the big, heavy blade that dug into the earth. It was hard work, but it had to be done. Survival depended on it.

Working hard in the fields

In the southern highlands of Tanzania, the cold winter months are June through September. Winter is primarily dry, with very little or no rain. Since I arrived in August, I saw evidence of drought everywhere I looked. Every surface was covered with a layer of *vumbi* (dust.) Even the leaves of trees and petals of flowers were disguised with brownish red dust. It was something I would have to get used to.

Pulling up to my new home was quite a thrill. The house looked like a little cabin. Mwasha and I went in to look around. I was surprised to see a whole group of villagers sitting in my house! There were four men and a woman. I was introduced to the village

95

chief, whose name was Huruma, and three of his government staff members. Frank Kinyonge, the headmaster of the primary school, was also there. He would be my counterpart, and we would work closely together. Frank spoke fairly good English and often helped me with the Swahili language. No one else in the village spoke English at all. When the chief spoke Swahili very fast, it was especially hard to follow the conversation. Frank was a big help with interpretation. I sat with these village leaders, and they served me a soda. (I learned later that this was the special drink of choice for guests!) *Chai* (tea) was drunk daily by villagers; soda was for company!

I cast my eyes around the space I would now call home. The floors and walls of the house were concrete, and the roof was made of tin, although it seemed to have pieces missing. The house had two good-sized bedrooms with a small living room. There was no running water or electricity. And there was dust on everything.

Mwasha told the chief and his council members that repairs needed to be made to my house. The door needed to be fixed, and new locks installed. He also noted that some of the ceiling boards were missing, and he wanted that fixed right away. On behalf of the Peace Corps, Mwasha wanted to be sure I was safe and as comfortable as possible. I was thankful for that. He said, "We want to make it right for Bibi Kay." The chief agreed, and arrangements were made for the repairs to be done.

I was thankful for Mwasha's insistence on these improvements. Even though I loved the passion fruit that grew outside my house, I didn't really appreciate the vines and leaves that actually grew under my tin roof and into my house. I could only imagine some of the other critters that could make themselves at home within my walls. A new ceiling would be nice.

The house had been vacant for two weeks and was dusty and needed a thorough cleaning. I spent a good deal of time scrubbing down the walls and getting rid of hundreds of cobwebs. Mwasha told me that the good news was, since it was cold and our village was at a high elevation, there probably wouldn't be any snakes in the house.

Out the back door was a small courtyard with three small, attached rooms. One was the kitchen, if you could call it that. There was a one burner propane *jiko* (stove). Most of the cooking would be done outside on a clay and metal *jiko* that used homemade charcoal for heat. There was also a brick fireplace in the corner of the courtyard. It was used when larger pots needed to be heated. One of the rooms was a sort of shower/bathing room. I would have to heat water on the kitchen *jiko* and carry it to the shower room if I wanted to bathe in anything but cold river water. The last little room was the *choo* (toilet). This was nothing more than a hole in the concrete floor, where I was expected to squat. There were actually depressions in the concrete where my feet were supposed to be placed for the most accurate aim. I immediately started making plans to improve the toilet situation. At the very least, I needed to be able to sit.

Although it was primitive, I was happy to call this little house my home. The Peace Corps volunteer who had lived there before me, Rachael Hocking, had started a wonderful garden with rows and rows of vegetables and flowers. There was an avocado tree shading the house and a passion fruit vine growing right up to the roof. Everything was in dire need of water, so one of the first things I did was to water the garden. I hired Nidaya to help me carry water from the *bomba* (faucet) that was located near the primary school, about one hundred yards from my house. It took three hours, but the roses, snapdragons and daisies were grateful.

I was fortunate that Rachael had left some of her furniture behind, so I had a bed and a table with a couple of chairs. She left me some clothes, too, which I really appreciated. She left me some

American skirts and some beautiful material that I would learn to drape over my slacks and wrap around my waist like the women in the village did. Peace Corps volunteers are expected to dress like the villagers so that we blend in as much as possible. There were two kinds of these 'skirts'. One, called a *kitenge*, was a colorful wrap. There was also a *kanga,* which was material that had symbolic spiritual writings along the lower edges. Wearing these skirts was a way of showing respect, so I was pleased that Rachael had thought of leaving them for me.

I found a Trek bicycle out in the courtyard. It had been given to Rachael by the PC, and she left it behind when she went back to the States. It didn't look like much, but it did work. I tried it out, riding circles in the courtyard. That bike would take me around the village in style!

One of the most valuable things she left me was a notebook that would help me get to know the village. She kept notes about the people and customs, as well as how she spent her days there. And she warned me to be careful if I went to the huge tree at the edge of the school soccer field, because it was home to a green *momba* (snake), which was extremely poisonous. Yes, Rachael's notes were very helpful!

When I talked to Frank about the green momba, he agreed that I should stay away from the tree where the snake lived. He told me they usually stayed high up in the tree branches, usually were not down on the ground, but they were highly poisonous. In fact, he said the green momba had been nicknamed 'the ten step snake.' When I questioned why they gave the snake that name, he told me it was because after a person was bitten, he could walk about ten steps before he fell down dead. I determined to keep my eyes open!

Rachael also left behind six hens and one rooster. They lived in a *kuku banda* (chicken coop) that Rachael had built for them. She also left several pigs, but I quickly gave them away. I didn't want those smelly pigs living so close to me. I planned to get some goats and rabbits, which would provide milk and meat.

I also inherited a mama cat and one of her kittens. They turned out to be great hunters and, in fact, the first evening in my new home I watched by candlelight as they stalked and caught two mice in my living room.

That first night in Uhekule was filled with mixed emotions. I was excited about the adventure that lay ahead, but also somewhat overwhelmed by the uncertainty of life in this foreign environment.

I sat at my little table and ate my supper, which consisted of an aluminum packet of smoked oysters that my daughter, Jill, had sent me in a 'care package' and some crackers that I brought along. I ate by candlelight, of course, but it was far from a romantic dinner! I could hear sounds outside, a few voices, insects, a baby crying. I heard a little rustling in the far corner of my house, and I wondered just how many mice had made their home in mine.

I looked around at the cement walls and made plans for cleaning the next day. I wondered if it would be possible to paint the whole interior of my house. It would be like a nice fresh start. I decided to ask Mwasha about that in the morning.

I thought about my family, back home in the United States, and prayed for them. I fell asleep that night, thanking God for the opportunity to be in Uhekule and asking for guidance and protection in the days ahead.

CHAPTER FOUR
Early Days

I had only been in Uhekule for a couple of days when I had to make the trip back to Dar es Salaam. Congresswoman McCullen from Minnesota was attending a meeting there and had expressed an interest in meeting me, a sixty-five-year-old Peace Corps volunteer with ties to Minnesota. So, after two days of cleaning and carrying water, I found myself on a bus headed out of the village.

The village 'bus,' if you can call it that, was barely held together by ropes and made for a wicked journey to town! The villagers told me it was 'the bus that sleeps in Uhekule.' I laughed and asked them to explain what it means. I learned that this bus made trips back and forth between Uhekule and Njombe, but that it always 'sleeps' in Uhekule. So, every morning, it was ready to return to Njombe town.

The trip to Njombe was about twenty-four kilometers and the roads were rough and dusty. We stayed the first night in Njombe and then traveled 12 more hours the next day to Dar es Salaam. This final leg of the journey was on a bigger, nicer bus, somewhat like a modern tour bus but certainly not as nice as a Greyhound bus back in the States. The roads were better, too, but the trip was still long and uncomfortable. Several other nearby PCVs met with Congresswoman McCullen that day. She had a photographer who documented her meeting with about twenty of us.

Needless to say, I was exhausted. After meeting with the congresswoman, I turned right around and made the trip home to Uhekule, by way of an overnight in Njombe.

While in Dar es Salaam, I learned that another volunteer, Sue Borah, who was a little older than me, would soon be leaving her village and returning to the United States. She had nearly finished her term of service in Ujindile, a village about twenty kilometers from Uhekule. She offered to sell me her furniture when she left. I heard that it was very nice furniture, well made by an excellent local craftsman. I agreed to buy what Sue couldn't take with her.

Frank Kinyonge, the headmaster of the primary school, was my nearest neighbor in Uhekule. He and his lovely, hardworking wife, Patricia, quickly became my friends. Frank knew good English, so it was nice to have him to talk with and learn from. I noticed a lot of children running in and out of their house, and one day I asked Frank how many children he had. He said, "Many!"

Frank became my mentor and bodyguard as well as friend. He was well respected in the village and helped me in many ways. Right from the start, I felt a kindred spirit with Frank and Patricia. We all seemed to understand the importance of education and advancement. Frank was my community counterpart, and we worked well together.

Frank took me on a little tour of the village. I walked through the primary school, a brick and cement building that didn't look like a comfortable place for learning. There were cracks in the walls and uneven, broken floors. In the center of each classroom were long rows of rough wooden tables and wooden chairs. I noticed that there were very few books in the room, and Frank explained that books were shared by two or three children at once. He also told me that the children never had homework, because when they got home from school they were expected to do chores. Also, the students were never allowed to take books home; they probably would never be returned to the school. I saw what looked like a chalkboard on one wall, but on closer inspection I learned that it was just black paint on the wall.

There were several classrooms like this, as well as an office area. Parents were required to provide a uniform for the children, as well as a paper notebook for writing exercises. Of course, there was no electricity, no running water or nice restroom, and no cafeteria. Frank explained that the parents 'paid' for school by providing *debes* (bushels) of corn and beans for the children to eat. The corn was taken to the mill and returned to the school as flour to make *ugali*. (a dough of corn flour and water cooked together.) Every meal at school consisted of *ugali* and beans. The villagers believed that *ugali* would make the children strong. Meals were prepared in a lean-to by a cook with the help of the seventh-grade students. The food was served on tin plates and the children went to the soccer field to sit on the grass and eat. When they were finished, they rinsed their plates and set them out in the sun to dry.

As I looked around the classrooms, I saw that the children were looking at me suspiciously. They had never seen an older white person before, and to them I was a bit frightening! Frank told them that I was not a ghost, but I'm not sure he convinced many of them.

The dispensary was in even worse condition than the school. There was a foundation but no walls. Cement partitions on the ground marked out where the rooms would be. But work on the construction had stopped because there was no money to continue. I saw this as a very important need. The villagers deserved better medical care. An operable dispensary was a must.

Frank told me about his wife's latest pregnancy. When Patricia's contractions started, they had to walk to the closest village, about six kilometers (or almost four miles) away. I could not imagine walking that far while having contractions! Everyone was surprised when, two hours later, Patricia delivered twins! Of course, there had been little or no prenatal care, and certainly no ultrasound to check for abnormalities. So, no one knew she was expecting twins.

I couldn't help but think back to my own pregnancy experiences. The clean and sterile hospital environment, the comfortable room where I could recover from the delivery, the attention of educated doctors and nurses, my own mother to give advice and childcare assistance—what a contrast to what Patricia and Frank had gone through.

My eyes wandered over this village, my new home. I saw poverty and hunger everywhere I looked. I saw cramped and dirty huts. I saw people doing back-breaking work and barely surviving. I saw orphans, sitting alone, desperate for some love and compassion. Already I was falling in love with these people. Already I was wondering how I could help them.

* * * * *

On September 17th. I was invited to a village meeting. It started at 9:30 am. The village chief and his council staff, Frank and I gathered in a small little office. I looked around the crowded room and realized that I was the only white person there, and I was also probably the oldest person there. Those two facts, as obvious as they were, would make me stand out in the village.

I was introduced to the group and then they wanted me to talk about myself. Frank helped me with the language as I told them about my reason for joining Peace Corps. After about an hour, we all went outside. A table and chairs were set up for the village leaders, Frank and me. Gathered around were about three hundred of the villagers, all sitting on the dusty grass. The men sat on one side, the women and babies sat on the other. I noticed that almost everyone sported very short hair; the men, women, boys and girls looked alike except for their clothing. The women and girls wore skirts; the men and boys wore long pants.

I was again asked to introduce myself to the group. As I stood and looked around at the eager faces of the villagers, I repeated the 'speech' I had given as my final language test in training. I told them all about myself, my family, how old I was, and how long I would be staying in Uhekule. I wanted to end the spiel with *"Nina penda Uhekule"* which means "I love Uhekule" but I forgot that very important part. 'Oh well,' I figured. 'I'll have plenty of other times I can tell them that.'

This meeting with the council members and the villagers lasted until 4:00 p.m. We had no food, no breaks and no water that whole time. It was a chilly day, and I wasn't prepared to sit out in the cold. In addition, my posterior was sore from sitting so long on a hard chair. Well, at least I wasn't sitting on the dusty ground.

CHAPTER FIVE
I Love Uhekule

Uhekule is supposedly better off than some of its neighboring villages. Yet everywhere I looked, poverty was obvious. Most of the homes were built of hand-made mud bricks and had dirt floors and thatched roofs. Some families were lucky enough to have cement floors and tin roofs. Almost every family had a small field of potatoes or corn. *Ngano* (wheat) was also raised. I only saw one farmer who used a plow pulled by an ox. Everyone else had to till the soil themselves. For the most part, the women and children worked in the fields. Men sat around talking, playing checkers or making *pombe* which was an alcoholic drink made from bamboo, similar to beer.

There were only a couple of motorized vehicles in Uhekule. I saw an old truck that might or might not actually run, and another broken down truck that most certainly wouldn't. The only vehicle that looked half-way operable was the bus that traveled to Njombe every few days. It wasn't the safest bus I'd ever ridden on, and lacked in comfort, but at least it worked.

Without vehicles to help with transporting goods, the villagers had to carry everything themselves. I was amazed at the burdens they could balance on their heads.

Although considered 'farmers', very few of the villagers raised animals. Some families had pigs, and there were only one or two cows. Chickens were everywhere, roaming free range. Cats were abundant and welcomed to keep down the mice and rats. *Simbilisi* (guinea pigs) were kept for food for the children. There wasn't much meat on a guinea pig, so adults didn't bother with eating them. It was just enough for a child, however.

In general, the nutrition of the villagers was lacking in protein. *Ugali* was served at every meal. It was a pasty-doughy mixture of corn flour and water, very starchy and to me mostly tasteless. Usually, the villagers would dip *ugali* into vegetable sauce made from locally grown vegetables. That did help with the taste a little. We ate rice and beans, eggs and vegetables like potatoes, tomatoes, onions and green peppers. Potatoes were readily available but other vegetables could be bought in town. Njombe had many *dukas* (small stands or shops) that sold local green vegetables like *mchicha* (spinach)and *figili* (celery). Many kinds of fruit grew in Uheluke village. Meat was only served once a week or on special occasions like holidays, weddings or funerals. I ate the chicken but stayed away from pork because it usually had pig hair left on it!

In the center of the village was a large water holding tank partially buried in the ground. As water came down from the mountain, it was piped into the holding tank, which was like a huge box made of cement. Anyone needing water would draw it from the *bomba* (faucets) scattered around the village and fill their buckets. Then they would carry the buckets to their homes, usually balanced on their heads.

The holding tank was cleaned monthly, but water still had to be boiled for cooking or drinking. In modernized societies, it's easy to take water for granted. Turn on a faucet and – ta-da- there's fresh, drinkable water. Even heated! But here in Uhekule, and in so many other places throughout the world, clean water is hard to come by. Water is essential for life, and yet requires an immense amount of effort to secure. I don't think most Americans have any idea about the amount of work required just to survive in many parts of the world.

The pipes carrying water down the mountain were about six inches in diameter. Sometimes, the pipes would clog with debris and the water would stop coming into the village. Someone would have to go hunting to find where the clog was, and then clean out the pipe. That meant an interruption in our water service.

When I carried buckets of water from the *bomba*, I stored it in a big barrel just outside my house, by the back door. I tried to make sure I never ran out of water. Unfortunately, all the trips back and forth to carry water to my house soon took a toll on my shoulders and back. I went to the village chief and asked for help. To my surprise, just a couple of days later, there were forty people digging a trench from the holding tank in the center of the village to my back yard. It was a distance of about two blocks, through yards, across fields and over a road. In no time at all, I had water piped right to a *bomba* (faucet) in my back yard.

The chief and most of the villagers showed me great respect. I learned that their older citizens were always held in high regard. And I was definitely in the category of 'older.' Before long, everyone was calling me '*Bibi Kay*' which means Grandma or Madam.

However, the babies and toddlers were not so quick to recognize me as a Bibi. It seemed that whenever I got close to a very young child, they would scream or cry. They would turn their faces away from me as if they couldn't stand to look at me. Sometimes they would hide behind their mother's skirts. It bothered me at first, but then I realized that they were reacting to me because of the color of my skin. I was a surprise, and they couldn't understand why I looked so different. I wanted so badly to hold the babies and soothe them, but instead I decided to just give them time to get used to me. Before long, as the adults became more accepting of me, the babies did, too. What joy I felt when the toddlers started walking to me with their arms outstretched, saying "Bibi, Bibi."

There was a dog who had wandered into my yard and started to think that he belonged to me. And I didn't mind; I had always loved dogs. I named him Shadow, and he was a wonderful companion. One day I was playing with Shadow and some of the school children were watching us from the fence. I threw a stick, and Shadow returned it to me. The children were intrigued. It seemed like, after that, they were more comfortable with me. I guess they thought that if I liked dogs, I must be a nice lady, despite my ghostly appearance!

Most of the adults were willing to help and learn from me. But for the first few months, Peace Corps volunteers are not supposed to do any 'teaching.' We were supposed to observe the community, access needs, and come up with ideas for making sustainable income generating projects.

I couldn't help myself, though. I knew that September is the month when New Castle Disease can wipe out all the chickens in a village, especially those that roam free. And Uhekule had lots of free-range chickens. Eggs were an important source of protein for the villagers, so I knew that it was important to keep the flocks healthy. I arranged for the Peace Corps to send me the vaccine I would need to protect the village chickens from the highly contagious New Castle Disease. We vaccinated 251 *kuku* by putting one drop of vaccine in the chicken's eye. I think I also vaccinated myself as one of the hens pecked me and I got a couple drops of vaccine in the open sore. I guess I won't have to worry about succumbing to New Castle Disease this year!

Vaccinating the *kukus* was a job I felt was necessary because of the threat of contagion. The rest of my early days in Uhekule, I poured my energies into trying to get to know the villagers. I also started to come up with a plan for how I could help them become more self-sufficient and healthier. I thought about beekeeping, which could provide honey for sale. I decided to invite a few of my neighbors to come to my courtyard to learn about making jam. I also knew it was important to write a grant to get the dispensary built and operational.

Yes, there was lots to do! As I settled into a routine, more and more ideas came to me. I had already fallen in love with the people here. Even the young children and little babies were starting to feel comfortable around me. I was forming relationships with many people in the village. And even though they lived in poverty like I had never seen before, they were willing to share what they had to make a stranger feel welcome. I had many opportunities to say, *"Nina penda Uhekule."* (I love Uhekule.)

CHAPTER SIX
Legal Matters

In mid-November, I took the bus to Njombe and connected to the internet at a small cafe. I opened up my email and saw that there was a letter from Floyd. He was asking for a divorce. He said he had met a woman he wanted to date, but she was not willing to date a 'married man.' We had been separated for almost two years, and I agreed that a divorce was clearly in our future. So, I told him that, yes, I would agree to the divorce, but that he was going to have to pay for it! He went along with that plan, and a large packet of papers was sent to me from his lawyer.

Unfortunately, Floyd's lawyer said that the papers needed to be signed, notarized and then returned to him. That might be a problem! How was I going to find a notary in Tanzania? Certainly not in Uhekule! It took a while, but I did eventually go to the courthouse in Njombe where there was a magistrate trying a criminal case. I left the papers with the magistrate's assistant and returned a couple of hours later. The judge had stamped and signed each page two or three times. I'm not sure she even knew what the document said! But the papers were signed, so I went to the post office and mailed them back to Minnesota. Our divorce was finalized in 2006.

Several months later, Floyd sent me a letter. He apologized for interrupting my work in Tanzania with the details of the divorce. "I'm sorry for bothering you with the divorce papers when you were so busy with your new life." He said he knew I wanted to focus on the important things I was doing there. We had both moved on to new endeavors.

CHAPTER SEVEN
Furniture Exchange

I took a trip to visit Sue Borah to pick up the furniture I bought from her. I hired a driver, Benjamin, who had a truck, to help load the items. The local *fundi* (craftsman) named Jerod, came along too. Jerod knew how to work with cement, and I wanted to show him something at Sue's house.

Sue lived in a really nice home, built years before by Danish missionaries. It was a far more modern house than any of the other Peace Corps volunteers lived in. The view of the mountains was absolutely breathtaking. I thought my views in Uhekule were beautiful, but this village was situated in an awesome setting.

As amazing as the views were, there was one quality of Sue's home that was even more impressive! This house had an up-to-date *choo!* (toilet)

I showed the *choo* to Jerod and explained my dream of modernizing my *choo* back in Uhekule. When Jerod understood my vision, he promised to get right to work. It was a new concept; no home in Uhekule had a fancy toilet like that! And, of course, the villagers had never traveled to the big cities so had no idea such luxuries existed. But Jerod was eager to build the first (somewhat modern) toilet in Uhekule.

My new furniture, bought from Sue Borah, was, as promised, an excellent quality. I bought two sofas, a nice table and chairs and another small table. I now could give my older furniture away.

Originally left behind by Rachael, it was decent furniture but nothing special.

Frank and I had already decided who to give my old furniture to. He had told me about a family in great need. The parents of three girls had died, leaving the oldest girl to care for her two sisters. She was only twenty-one and had been doing her best for three years. Their home had an outside kitchen and a 6x8 foot room with no furniture. They all slept on the dirt floor. To say the situation was sad is an understatement.

I gave them my old sofa and a matching chair. Frank and I were concerned that the girls might decide to sell the furniture to get some badly needed money. But we went back to visit them a few weeks later, and they still had the furniture, so we were relieved. They were no longer sleeping on the floor.

I often took the girls eggs from my *kukus* (chickens) and did what I could to help them out. When I thought of how poor some of the villagers were, and how hard they had to work just to survive, it nearly broke my heart. I was determined to do my best to give them some skills to improve their conditions.

CHAPTER EIGHT
The Importance of Education

I believed that education would be one of the best ways out of poverty. Looking at the condition of the primary school, I knew something needed to be done to improve the chances of a good education. Frank was doing the best he could, but his resources were limited. Surely, I could help.

The primary school, kindergarten through grade seven, had 431 students. There were seven teachers, meaning the average class size was about sixty students. The children wore uniforms – a white blouse or shirt topped with a green sweater and blue skirts or pants. I could tell that most of the clothes had been handed down through the families because everything was tattered. Some of the sweaters could better be described as green yarn draped over the shoulders – they were in really bad shape. Skirts and pants had holes, too. Often the school uniforms were worn all day, every day. I saw children wearing school uniforms at church. It was quite likely the only clothes the children had for good.

Of the total enrollment, nearly one-third of the children were orphans. An orphan in Tanzania is any child who had lost one or both of his or her parents. The number of orphans in itself was overwhelming. Children without parents often lived with relatives in extremely crowded situations. Food insecurity, mental health issues, and a sense of hopelessness often clouded any chances for learning.

I learned of one little girl whose name was Eliza. Both of her parents died with AIDS. She went to live with her aunt in my village.

While there, she was treated as second class, even by her family. She was not allowed to go to school. She stayed home to do chores and care for the younger children. Frank, the headmaster of the school, came to talk to me about Eliza's situation. We both wanted to get Eliza into school. We confronted the aunt, but she refused. It made me so upset, but there wasn't much I could do.

Frank told me that the government is moving away from putting children in orphanages. The preferred placement is in Foster Care. The problem with that, of course, is that there are thousands of orphans, and only a small number of foster families. So, many children are left homeless or live in situations such as Eliza's. At least she had a roof over her head, and food from time to time.

Diseases such as tuberculosis and malaria had moved through the village, but the most prevalent cause of death was HIV/AIDS. Peace Corps provided trainings on AIDS prevention, and I knew that part of my reason to be in Uhekule was to share that information with the villagers.

It soon became clear to me that much of my time in Uhekule would be spent on education and health. But I also wanted to encourage self-sufficiency and entrepreneurship. My first endeavor in that direction was to teach jam making, with the hopes that maybe eventually it could become a business and provide a new source of income for the village.

CHAPTER NINE
Daily Life

I decided that I could accomplish more of my Peace Corps duties if I had someone to help me with cooking and cleaning. Frank knew of a young woman who was desperate for some work. He thought she would be perfect for the job. So, I hired this young woman to help me with chores around the house. Her name was Shukuru and she was just eighteen years old. I called her my house daughter, and she was just wonderful. Her father had died from HIV/AIDS when she was only twelve, and then her mother died two years later. That left Shukuru as head of household for three younger brothers. She was a hard worker and had managed somehow to care for the brothers for four years before I offered her a job with me. Their home was made of mud bricks and had a dirt floor. In one room, the two oldest boys slept on a foam mattress placed on the floor. In the small bedroom, Shukuru and the youngest brother, Noeli, slept on another piece of foam. It was a meager existence, for sure, and I would be able to help this family by offering Shukuru a job.

Cooking meals in Uhekule often took all day. No microwaves or gas ovens here! The villagers had a fascinating way of cooking over an open fire in their homes. First three large rocks were placed on the ground. Between each rock a long thick log was laid on the ground, making a star shape, with an open space in the middle. A fire was lit in that open space and burned the ends of the logs. As the wood burned, the logs were pushed into the circle further and further. That way the fire never went out. A *sufuria* (cooking pot) that balanced on the rocks, was placed over the flames. I thought it was an ingenious way of cooking!

Usually, these fires were on the floor inside the homes. I found it very difficult to breathe in all the smoke that was created. I could never stay inside the building for more than a minute or two when the fire was burning. Even when the cooking was finished, the smell of the smoke lingered.

Rachael had built a brick fireplace in the corner of my courtyard, near the fence. It was well made and proved to be a great place for cooking, especially when using larger pots.

I also had a small clay and metal stove, called a *jiko,* that was like a small Weber grill but not as nice. I could use it outside in my courtyard because it was heated by chunks of home-made charcoal. Propane would be used when cooking inside. The propane *jiko,* with its one burner, was usually kept in my small kitchen. Every day was an adventure in cooking. I was grateful for Shukuru's help.

Shukuru also helped with laundry. That was another chore that could take a whole day. We set up four big buckets of water in the courtyard. Clothes were dipped into hot water, sloshed up and down with a bar of soap to remove most of the dirt, and then rinsed in the other three buckets. They would be spread on a line to dry. If anything needed to be ironed, Shukura used an iron that reminded me of one my grandmother would have used. She put home-made charcoal into the iron and set it on a grate to heat up. We did iron my blouses, but usually nothing else.

As you may imagine, dental health was not important to the villagers. In fact, hygiene in general was barely given a thought. Everyone ate with their fingers, and no one thought to wash first. No one knew about forks and spoons or soap and toothbrushes. I made a rule that anyone eating in my house would wash their hands first and use a spoon, not their fingers. Shukuru caught on quickly, but most people looked at me like I was crazy. Old habits are hard to break.

I noticed that Shukuru had some teeth that looked bad. I decided to take her to a dentist in Njombe. She had two large cavities and two smaller ones. The dentist did a great job, and it cost nearly nothing - $8.00 in US currency!

CHAPTER TEN
Sustainability

I bought a toilet seat when I was in Dar, and Jerod got busy on the *choo*. He built a cement enclosure to surround the hole in the floor of the *choo*. I had the honor of fitting the toilet seat onto the top while the cement was wet. Jerod was a perfectionist and followed my directions precisely. He made it at the correct height, and I couldn't have asked for better. It was amazing! For two months, I had managed to 'aim carefully' but now - no more squatting! I could actually sit down in comfort!

Jerod was so proud of his work, he decided to make a sit-down *choo* for himself! He invited his neighbors to come see the fancy new toilet and soon he was building them for other villagers. Jerod had discovered a new source of income and a new business enterprise for himself. That's what Peace Corps means by 'sustainability', and it came about through my own personal need.

It was time to introduce some of the women to the idea of sustainability, too. I was overjoyed when nine of the mamas came to my courtyard to help me make papaya jam. We worked long and hard, cooking the fruit over the fire in my courtyard, and we filled twelve jars. It was a beginning. I had hopes to continue, with a variety of fruits, and eventually find a way to sell jam in town or maybe even in one of the larger cities. It could be a way for the women to supplement their meager income.

Unfortunately, sugar was expensive! I provided the sugar for that first batch of jam, but I knew that the villagers would not be able to afford it on their own in the future. So much for sustainability! We would have to come up with another way to sweeten our jam. I wondered if honey would work. I made plans to investigate beekeeping.

For the next couple of months, the mamas and I continued our jam making. We experimented with different fruits and came up with six very agreeable flavors. I also taught them how to make banana cake – a really nice treat!

None of these jam-makers have ever been very far outside of Uhekule Village, and the economy in any of the surrounding villages would not really support a large or profitable jam business. So, marketing our jam was left up to me. I got my first big opportunity when I traveled to Dar es Salaam in November. I met with the food and beverage manager of the Holiday Inn, the fanciest hotel in Dar. I took twelve jars of mango jam – and sold them all! I knew the mamas would be so happy to have this little income, and I hoped that the hotel would be contacting me for further orders of jam in the future. Already I could see that this would be a good project to continue. We would need to find a less expensive source of sweetness, and we would have to secure transportation to deliver the jam to the hotels or wherever we managed to do business. There were lots of details to work out. Time would tell where all this would lead.

Thanksgiving was spent in Dar es Salaam at the home of the US ambassador. He had invited all 130 of the Peace Corps volunteers to celebrate the holiday with him, and almost all of us attended. It was a twelve-hour bus ride for me, but worth it! I enjoyed meeting up with some of the 'kids' I had gone through training with. I hadn't seen them in the three months since our swearing in ceremony.

As I strolled around the Ambassador's beautiful home and manicured grounds, I took in the grandeur of his lifestyle and contrasted it to the sad poverty in Uhekule. The Ambassador's house was huge, and decorated with the finest of furnishings, expensive art, and beautiful touches. I thought of my new friends, living in spaces smaller than the closets in this mansion. I remembered the orphaned girls who slept in the dirt for years before I gave them a hand-me-down sofa. Outside this decadent home, the gardens were well tended, and seating areas had been arranged to optimize the view of the Indian Ocean. It was a beautiful place to sit with a beverage and relax. I thought of the villagers back in Uhekule, sitting outside in the dust for hours, with nothing to drink but water or chai and no time to relax. The contrast saddened me.

Tanzania was the fifth poorest country in the world, with people dying every day from starvation, disease and AIDS. To see the American Ambassador living comfortably in this elaborate showcase of a home – well, it didn't seem right.

The Thanksgiving meal was wonderful, I must admit. We had turkey and all the trimmings, and I ate well. Wine and beer flowed freely, served by a wait-staff dressed in clean white uniforms. Again, I thought about the Uhekule school students dressed in rags. I hoped that something I did in my next two years would provide a better way of life for the villagers who were already becoming like family to me.

Before we left the Ambassadors' party, he encouraged each of us to take a bag or two of little McDonald's Happy Meal toys back to the children in our villages. (Apparently the Ambassador owned several McDonald's businesses.) I was the last PCV to leave the party, and when I went into the spacious dining room to gather my bags of toys, I saw that there were at least fifty bags remaining! Well, I took fourteen! I had to make several trips out to the car, but

I couldn't help but think of the joy these little toys would bring to the children of Uhekule.

I had never seen the village children playing with any actual toys. Sometimes they made their own balls out of plastic bags, rolled up and tied with twine. Mostly they played with sticks or an old bicycle wheel. Whatever they could make into a toy, they used. Once I saw an old rubber flip-flop and part of a plastic jug turned into a sort of automobile with the tires made from the flip-flops. I'm sure none of the children had ever had a store-bought toy. Even dolls were rare, and of course, were made of rags. But this year, they would get some cute toys for Christmas. I could already imagine the happy faces.

While I was there with the Ambassador, I told him of my hopes for starting a jam making business with the mamas in the village. He seemed interested in the project and even bought a jar of jam I had brought along, intending as a gift for him. He insisted on paying for it, and even paid more than double what we normally asked for a jar. When I got back to the village, I wrote to him, asking for his help with marketing in the city. My hopes were high – between my contacts with the Ambassador and the food manager at the Holiday Inn, I hoped that the jam business would take off. The women of Uhekule could certainly use the cash.

CHAPTER ELEVEN

Lessons

I believe the Uhekule women had an inborn knack for securing their kitenges and kanga. No matter how I tried to tuck them around me like the villagers did, I just couldn't seem to make them stay on. The mamas showed me the proper way to secure them, but whenever I did it myself, it wasn't long before the skirt was falling off of me! The ladies would break out in a laugh, then someone would run over to assist me one more time. Finally, I just gave up! I tucked the material into the waistband of my slacks and decided that was good enough.

There are five denominations of churches in Uhekule – Catholic, Lutheran, Pentecostal, Assembly of God and 7th Day Adventist. I visited all the churches except the 7th Day Adventist, because they met on Saturday, and I was always busy or traveling. Frank went with me when I visited each church.

Whenever I visited a church for the first time, I always brought a small gift. I bought a few small vases when I was in Njombe and fixed a little arrangement of local flowers to present to the pastor. Then Frank and I would sit in the back row, so I could better observe the service.

On the day we visited the Pentecostal Church, Frank and I noticed that many parishioners were standing along the wall, facing it, crying at the tops of their voices. I looked at Frank and asked, "Why are they doing that?" to which he responded, "I have no idea!" He was Lutheran, so this was all new to him, too.

I felt most comfortable with the Lutherans, because I thought their service was most like the Methodist Church I attended back home. There were some big differences, however. The services usually lasted two or three hours. I will admit, many times I could not keep up with the Swahili. It was a struggle to understand what was being said, especially when the pastor spoke fast. I just couldn't translate in my mind that quickly and I knew I was missing most of the message. So, I learned to bring along something to read. My friend Joan sent me a paperback book written by former Peace Corps volunteers, telling about their experiences. I would slip it inside my Bible, so it looked like I was studying the scriptures. But really, I was reading a good book in English!

After the preaching and singing, we all went outside. We had a prayer and then they held an auction! People who could not afford a cash offering would bring in things to sell – potatoes, other vegetables, homemade soap – and they would be sold to the highest bidder. There was an older villager, Mr. Lutangano, who often bid on items and then gave them to me. As he purchased potatoes, he would say "*Viazi kwa* Bibi Kay." I was amazed, once again, at the generosity of these people.

Early in December, I had the opportunity to teach Frank's class of sixth graders. I told them about myself, I showed them on the map where I came from, and I explained a little about life in America. I ended by showing them a potato masher, a common kitchen implement in the United States, but one they had never seen before. Potatoes are a main crop in Uhekule and are usually eaten boiled or baked. The villagers had never experienced mashed potatoes.

I decided that, when school convened after Christmas, I would ask each of the children to bring a potato to class. Then I will bring my *jiko* (charcoal stove) to the school, and we will make mashed potatoes. What fun we could have!

While I was with the school children, I also tried to teach them about the importance of good hygiene. I encouraged them to wash their hands often, especially before eating. I brought some dental floss from the US and showed the students how to floss their teeth. They were very attentive and respectful, but I knew it was going to take more than an hour of instruction to change years of bad habits. It was worth it to try, though.

CHAPTER TWELVE
Bigger Projects

In December, Frank and I traveled to Morogoro and spent the night there with several other volunteers from my class. We were headed for Tanga, specifically the Amani region, for additional PCV training. There were fourteen volunteers and their counterparts who attended this three-day training. We were put up in a lodge in the rain forest. I almost felt like I was on vacation. The trees and foliage were unbelievably lush and beautiful. We were served delicious meals of rice and chicken with vegetables every day. It was nice to be fed so well, and it was also good to see some of my former classmates. The setting, food and fellowship made the long bumpy travel days more bearable.

The purpose of this in-service training was to learn about writing grants. Volunteers would be requesting funding and support for some of the larger projects we wanted to work on during our stay in Tanzania. I had determined that one of the most pressing needs in Uhekule was for completion of the dispensary. It needed more than a floor! (And even then, the foundation was already in bad shape.) The nearest village with a dispensary was about four miles away. The Uhekule villagers really needed their own dispensary, and I wrote a grant to procure funding for finishing the building. Then my real work would begin.

CHAPTER THIRTEEN
Christmas

My first Christmas in Uhekule was certainly different – no decorated trees, no Santas, no carols piped through shopping centers, no presents. There was no money for gift buying, of course, but the villagers didn't need wrapping paper and surprises to celebrate the holiday. The emphasis was truly on the reason for the season.

Church on Sunday, Christmas Day, was three hours long. I sat on a hard wooden bench for the whole time, wishing I had brought along a pillow or blanket to cushion my bottom.

The next day, Boxer Day, we had church again and that time the service lasted four hours. The villagers celebrated the birth of the Christ child, focusing on the miracle of the Holy birth. There was singing and preaching, and the feeling was one of great joy. I appreciated this emphasis on the real reason for Christmas, rather than the commercial and secular focus that had been prevalent in the United States.

Afterwards, we had a nice meal of rice and beans together. I gave the McDonald's toys to the children, and, of course, they showed their appreciation with smiles. It warmed my heart seeing those children so excited and joyful over the receipt of just a little McDonald's happy meal toy. I thought about children in more 'civilized' countries, where dozens of presents sit under the Christmas tree, opened and set aside as the kids tear into the next package. I was thankful to be among these children who were so grateful for the tiniest of gifts.

I received a gift myself. Peace Corps delivered a bicycle to me, an unexpected surprise. I already had the bike that Rachael had left behind, so at first, I was willing to give the new one back, thinking that another volunteer might need it more than me. But the driver insisted that I keep it, and I realized that it would possibly come in handy in the future.

Care packages from the United States arrived, too. I so appreciated the gifts of snack foods like crackers and nuts. My son, Jon, and his wife, Betsy, sent several packages of Tuna Creations by Star-Kist – what a feast I had! I was also sent some gardening gloves and packages of vegetable seeds. My friend, Joan Anderson, from Minnesota even sent me a pair of TEVA shoes. Everything was helpful, and I was glad for the gifts. It was especially nice to know I had not been forgotten.

That first Christmas, away from family and home, was not as difficult as I thought it might be. I missed everyone, of course, but was kept busy with my new friends. As I lay in my bed that Christmas night, I thanked God for bringing me to Uhekule and providing the means to serve and help the villagers. I had been in Africa for six months. Already my experiences had impacted my life.

CHAPTER FOURTEEN
Visitors

I worked hard on my grant proposal for building the dispensary/ clinic. It was so important to get that building up and operational. I felt it was a very worthwhile project for the Peace Corps to be a part of. The proposal was nearly complete when I had a visitor.

Diane Solmonson, a missionary from Minnesota, was studying in Iringa. She was training under a partnership program with the Lutheran Church in Maple Grove, Minnesota. I had never met her before, but she was a friend of my best friend in Minnesota. We connected for a day and a night in Njombe and had a great time visiting. She instantly became my 'sister,' (although it might have been better described as a mother/daughter relationship, because of our ages.)

When Diane came, she brought me many gifts from the United States. Care packages were always appreciated, of course, but this was extra special. She gave me forty bars of Dial soap! What a treasure that was! She also brought a beautiful prayer shawl. When I wrapped it over my shoulders, I could almost feel the comfort of people back in Minnesota who were supporting me with their prayers.

I left Njombe and traveled twelve hours to Dar es Salaam. There I had a very special visitor, Michael Moriarty from Hot Springs Village, Arkansas. We spent three days on Zanzibar Island enjoying good food, snorkeling and beautiful white beaches. Zanzibar was known as the 'spice capital,' and we visited a spice farm, where an amazing variety of spices were grown. The production of cloves was one of the biggest industries in Zanzibar. It was a wonderful get-away, and over much too quickly.

After our little vacation, we returned to Dar es Salaam so I could go to the Peace Corps office to deliver my grant proposal. I also needed to see Dr. Jean Luc, the Peace Corps doctor. He checked me over and announced that I had lost twenty-five pounds since arriving six months earlier. I wasn't surprised by that; my clothes were practically falling off me – and not just my *kitenges!*

I asked Dr. Luc to check the bottom of my foot – I had been having trouble walking – there was a painful area that I thought was a corn. "Not a corn," he said. "A jigger (chigger)." He removed a worm about 1/4 of an inch long, full of eggs. No wonder it hurt to walk! In training we had been told never to go barefoot and to wear full shoes, not sandals. Now I knew why.

Michael and I traveled to Uhekule, and he stayed until March 12. We had a good time riding bicycles to Ujindile Village to visit another Peace Corps volunteer. It was a round trip of forty-six kilometers (just under thirty miles.) I was thankful to have two bikes to use. Unfortunately, the volunteer we were going to see was not there. She had gone to Dar for medical reasons. Of course, there was no way for us to call ahead to be sure she would be home. Telephones – another thing we in the 'modern world' take for granted. Our flip-phones did not always work.

I continued to work in the village while Michael was there, so he had a lot of time on his hands. He played many games of Sudoku! He told me he was getting a little bored because "No one here speaks English!"

We made plans for Michael to return for another visit in six months or so. Peace Corps allows volunteers to have visitors, but they can only stay for thirty days at a time. I was glad that Michael was willing to make that long trip, even though he felt out of place amongst people who didn't speak English!

CHAPTER FIFTEEN
Fun and Games

I spent a great deal of time with the children of Uhekule. I could watch them from my house as they walked to school and while they ate lunch on their soccer field. One of the things I noticed was that they really loved playing together on Sunday afternoons. I bought them a soccer ball, and they would come over to politely ask for it so they could play 'football.' They played barefoot on a field of grass that was about a foot tall. And they would play for hours and hours. I'm sure they hadn't eaten for a long time, but that didn't keep them from their 'football game.' I loved to watch them play, and sometimes I would join them. Even though the play got rough sometimes, there was no fighting or yelling – just laughter and fun!

The boys and girls in primary school loved my dog Shadow. They quickly learned how to say his name and called out to him whenever they saw him. Shadow was so good with them. He enjoyed the attention and all the pets they gave him. When the children called him from the schoolyard, he went eagerly to play with them.

The children knew I kept a stash of *pipi* (candy), but they quickly learned not to ask for it. Instead, they would ask if I had any chores for them to do. They knew I would pay them in candy.

The villagers did like their sugar, and not just candy. Whether it was a cola drink, some sweetened tea or a cane of pure sugar, they all loved sugar. That, along with limited calcium intake and almost non-existent dental hygiene, led to a lot of tooth decay.

One day I took Shukuru's twelve-year-old brother on a bike ride to Makoga, seven kilometers (about three miles) away. The 'dentist' there extracted a molar that had a big cavity. He used no Novocain, yet there were no tears. These villagers are tough, even the children. They are used to hard work and pain. They do not complain. I felt bad that I didn't take him to Njombe to see a real dentist and have the molar filled. But if I did that for everyone needing dental care, I would accomplish nothing else.

CHAPTER SIXTEEN
Life and Death in Uhekule

It makes sense that diseases can run rampant through the villages. Cleanliness and sanitation are almost foreign concepts. Insect and snake bites lead to malaria and death. Pure water was not always available. Simplest hygiene routines were not practiced.

One of the PCV's had just returned from a medical visit in Dar. I learned that he had intestinal round worms. Ugh! I had that chigger worm removed from my foot and learned how to do it myself. Unfortunately, I had to practice that skill several times

I could never be certain exactly what I was eating. I had several bouts of diarrhea. Once, when I was in Njombe, I passed out for a few minutes. I was taken to the medical clinic and tests were run. The doctor diagnosed me with malaria. Because of my background in medical lab work, I asked to see the blood samples for myself. I studied the slides under a microscope. I knew what malaria would look like, and my samples did not indicate malaria.

While I was in the hospital in Njombe, I learned about the level of care patients received, or it might be better called 'level of neglect.' I was given no food or water. I had to buy my own water or *kahawa* (coffee). The only thing I had to eat while I was there was when a friend brought me *a chapati*, which was a small flat bread with sugar sprinkled on top.

I was glad when I left the hospital. I went home, ate some vegetables and beans, rested and was just fine the next day. I never did find out why I had passed out. But it wasn't malaria – even though that's what the doctors there said. Even the 'trained' medical personnel in Njombe could not always be trusted for a correct diagnosis.

Not only were diagnoses often questionable, but the old traditions and beliefs in the 'bush' were often more harmful than the actual condition itself. One day, I heard a horrifying story. It involved a witch doctor. Old time superstitions held great power over the villagers and witch doctors were both feared and trusted. I heard about a man who visited a witch doctor and said he wanted to be rich. He asked the witch doctor what he could do to become a rich man. He was told to put his face in a pot of boiling water. The witch doctor said that would make him rich, and foolishly, the man believed him. What followed was intense pain, and no wealth.

Witch doctors often insisted that their 'cures' would work, but when the 'patient' did what was suggested, they would come back worse than before. I heard of a case when the witch doctor gave a 'remedy' to stop a pregnancy, but the young woman died from the procedure. The power these witch doctors held over some of the villagers was undeniable and frightening. Education was badly needed to overcome these superstitions and provide better options.

Villagers with HIV/AIDS were often embarrassed about their condition and didn't want to own up to it. Even when someone died from AIDS, it wasn't acknowledged as such. People would call it pneumonia, malaria or TB. They didn't want to talk about AIDS, its cause, prevention or treatment. One day a young woman, just twenty-three, died. I was so surprised to hear some of the village women talking about it and stating that she had died from AIDS. I was thrilled that they spoke so candidly with me about it. Slowly, the villagers were beginning to be a little more open with a discussion about AIDS. I started to make plans to hold a weeklong HIV/AIDS seminar in May.

This disease is so devastating, and the villagers needed to understand it better. Young girls, who desperately wanted to get an education, would sleep with the truckers, coming up from the south, for money to pay the school tuition. Unfortunately, they often became infected with AIDS – and there went their hopes for the future. It was a sad situation. Education would surely help curtail this epidemic.

I was reminded almost daily of the work that needed to be done for the dispensary. I sent requests for additional funding to all my friends and contacts in the United States. Money began to come in, over $1,500 in the first month. I thought about my fundraising experience with the church in Minnesota and realized that it had been a 'first step' towards this fundraising in Africa. Once again, I felt that God had been preparing me in so many facets of my life so that my time in Africa would be fruitful.

Since there was so much sickness and death in the village, I attended many funerals. Because there was no embalming, bodies had to be buried within twenty-four hours. Money was collected monthly throughout the villages to provide for the burials. Sometimes people paid their share with rice and vegetables.

I hadn't been in Uhekule long before I was told that I was expected to attend the funeral for a three-year-old girl named Polesano. This curious little child had pushed a chair up to a big barrel of water to look inside. She had leaned too far forward and fallen in and drowned. The girl who was supposed to be caring for her, was not watching carefully. After the funeral, people gathered at her home for a period of grieving. As we entered the house, we had to remove our shoes. A mat of woven weeds was spread out on the floor to provide a place for mourners to sit. The room was crowded with people crying and wailing in despair. As the mourners entered the house, they would shake hands with the grieving family members and say *"Pole sana."* (So sorry.) Then the cries of anguish started up again. It was a difficult scene.

This grieving could last for days and days, especially if the deceased person was well known or an important official in the village. Sometimes mourners were bussed in from other villages or towns.

After a long time of expressing grief, a meal was prepared. The usual funeral meal consisted of chicken, rice, and *kachumbari* (a salad made with tomatoes, onions and carrots with lemon juice, salt and pepper.) Everyone ate well. One of my PCV friends once told me funerals were well attended because the mourners always expected they would be well fed!

Another funeral I attended was for a little girl, Stella, who had cancer. She was a sixth grader, just twelve years old. She had been to Ikonda hospital located about seventy kilometers from Uhekule. where they had decided to amputate her right leg between her thigh and her knee. She lay in her hospital bed for three months after the surgery, lonely and sad. Finally, she was released from the hospital, put on a bus and sent home. She went back to school on crutches. Then the cancer came back, so she returned to the hospital. After another lonely stay, she was sent by bus to Makoga, a bumpy two-hour bus ride. Then she transferred to the Uhekule bus. When she arrived in Uhekule, they put her on the back of a bicycle to travel to her home. It saddens me to think how difficult those months had been for poor Stella. Painful and frightened only begin to describe what she must have been feeling. She died at home, the very next day.

The wake started a few hours after her death. When I learned about her passing, Shukuru and I rode bikes to her home. We took off our shoes at the door and went in. There in this dirty little room lay Stella. It was so hard to look at her little body, laid on a small bed and covered from head to toe with a blanket, and see the flat empty place where her right leg should have been. I left quickly and wept all the way home.

I couldn't help but think how different these outcomes would have been if proper medical attention was available. Education and accessibility – these two aspects of medical care became very important to me. And as I attended more and more funerals, I became more determined than ever to get our dispensary built.

CHAPTER SEVENTEEN
Jamming, Gardening and Growing Relationships

Our jam making endeavors continued. The peach trees were providing delicious peaches, and we were able to make thirty-seven jars of jam! It had proven to be a profitable project, and I established an arrangement with several hotels and restaurants in Dar.

We experimented with other ways of sweetening the jam but decided that only the real brown sugar was working. That meant that I would have to provide the sugar, at least until the 'business' started showing enough profit for the women to afford to buy it.

Whenever you put ten or twelve Uhekule women together, there was bound to be a lot of talking. Sometimes there was more gossiping going on than cooking. One day I walked out into my courtyard to see how the fruit cooking was going. The women were using the fireplace in the corner and cooking the peaches in a large pot. But they were deeply engaged in a conversation, and no one seemed to be paying attention to the fireplace. They didn't realize that the flames had leapt out and caught my fence on fire. I was not happy, but no serious damage was done. And I hoped the women got the message – it's important to pay attention while cooking!

Some of the Jam Mamas ready to sell their jam

Before long, we had mastered jam making. We had a variety of flavors: peach, mango, pineapple, plum and papaya. One day I was walking with some of the women and spotted a rhubarb plant. I was excited and said we could make jam with the rhubarb plant. The women disagreed with me, saying it was just *maua* (a flower). I explained that the stalk could be eaten, and they were skeptical but willing to try it. It took quite a bit of sugar, but the rhubarb jam was a hit.

As our jam making continued, I found that the women were more and more willing to open up to me about their worries and concerns. The day they first told me about an HIV death was a real turning point. Usually no one spoke of the disease. Those who were ill kept to themselves and didn't want anyone to know. HIV was a silent epidemic, and no one talked about it. For my jam-making mamas to discuss it with me was a real breakthrough. It lit a fire in me, and I wanted to do something substantial to slow the spread of the disease. I knew I wanted to write a grant for HIV education, and I determined that I was going to do what I could on a small scale even before the grant went through.

There was a small plot of land, about 40x20 feet, outside my courtyard. It sat vacant, and I had a plan. I asked the village council if I could have the land to make an HIV Victory Garden. I wanted to encourage the villagers with AIDS to eat better, with a variety of healthy vegetables. I hoped I could help these infected people work towards better health. I also hoped that, as we worked together in the garden, I could talk with them about their condition and how to prevent its spread. The village chief said I could have the land, but not to get my hopes up. He said people were too embarrassed to admit they had AIDS, and no one would come.

It was worth a try! And at first, I thought he was probably right. When I talked to the people, no one seemed interested. No one wanted to let it be known that they were HIV positive. No one would commit to helping me. So, I started it on my own.

As I worked away, clearing the brush and tilling the soil, I was surprised, (or should I say, overjoyed?) to see a man and a few women coming towards me. They were all HIV positive, but willing to step out and work with me. They were carrying buckets of 'fertilizer' on their heads to add to the dirt. Chicken droppings, I soon learned, made excellent fertilizer!

That was the beginning of our HIV Victory Garden. Our group was small but mighty. We planted carrots, and oh my goodness they did grow! We soon had a fabulous harvest of gorgeous carrots eight to ten inches long. We also had a good crop of *mchicha* (spinach).

A small step in the right direction is still progress.

The Victory Garden with a crop of huge carrots.

CHAPTER EIGHTEEN
Bigger Steps

In March of 2006, I attended an HIV/AIDS workshop in Mafinga for a week. It was presented by Dr. Delem from Peace Corps. The workshop was part of PEPFAR – the President's Emergency Plan for AIDS Relief. First announced by President George W. Bush in 2003, the program provided funding for treatment, prevention education and support in fourteen focus countries, Tanzania being one.

Sixteen Peace Corps Volunteers and their counterparts (host country nationals) were at this meeting. It was wonderful to reconnect with some of the 'kids' I had trained with. I was impressed with how their knowledge and dedication had increased just in the nine months we had been in Tanzania. They had wonderful stories to tell of their experiences. I saw their compassion, sensitivity and endurance and was amazed by each of them.

The younger PCVs treated me like an equal, even though there was an age difference of forty years or more. We socialized and joked around like peers, and we worked like the teammates we were. Much had already been accomplished in our villages, and we were all eager to get back to share the information from the HIV/AIDS workshop.

During one of the workshop sessions, I was asked if I knew how to prevent AIDS. My answer brought a chuckle from the other PCVs. "Yes, I do," I said. "The men need to keep their zippers zipped up!"

There were four guest speakers during the conference. Each of them had tested HIV positive. Their stories were eye opening as well as sad. Poverty, lack of education and sub-par medical care made the problem of HIV/AIDS widespread. No wonder President Bush wanted to help curtail this epidemic.

Overall, the workshop was informative, but I knew we had a huge job ahead of us. I started grant writing to secure some funds for AIDS education in Uhekule.

While I was attending the conference, I got word that progress was being made on the dispensary. Much *kazi* (work) had been done, even while I was away. The villagers had laid about eight-hundred meters of PVC pipe which would bring water into the dispensary. This was a very good first accomplishment!

Huruma, the village chairman, sent me a phone text to tell me the surprise. I was so glad that the villagers had participated in this improvement to their community. It was nice, even essential, to have their involvement. I could see that they were grateful for what Peace Corps was doing for them, and they wanted to be a part of it.

After the HIV conference, I stopped in Njombe on the way home, as usual. I arranged for a lori to pick up one-hundred bags of cement to have them delivered to Uhekule. I rode along with them – a free ride for me!

After they unloaded the cement, the lori driver and several villagers traveled around to other villages, picking up rocks that we could use for the foundation of the dispensary. The rocks were pounded by hand into stones that would help hold the cement floors intact. The old handmade bricks that were made for the foundation of the dispensary were not going to hold up the cement floor, so we needed something stronger. Rock would do the trick to keep the floors from cracking.

Once again, I marveled at the position I had been put in, and the way God had prepared me for this new chapter of my life. Who would ever imagine that, at age sixty-six, I would be working as a volunteer general contractor in Tanzania, Africa! Yet my experience with the church built in Minnesota had prepared me to be doing just that!

CHAPTER NINETEEN

PEPFAR in Action

Under PEPFAR (the President's Emergency Plan for AIDS Relief), US taxpayers provide fifteen billion dollars which is divided into fifteen countries. Thirteen of those countries are in Africa. I presented my seven-page grant proposal and was awarded a small amount of funding to educate my villagers. The money would provide speakers, nurses who would do voluntary AIDS testing, and lots of food for the conference.

In May, we held a weeklong *ukimwi* (AIDS) seminar. The primary speaker was Douglas Kisunga. He was a former teacher who had now dedicated his life to AIDS education. He was also HIV positive, so he had a lot of personal information to share.

On Monday, Bwana Kisunga and two other speakers explained the program to the village government. The training actually began on Tuesday. Because there are six sub-villages in Uhekule, we split them into three groups, with each group having a day long educational program. Those were held on Tuesday, Wednesday and Thursday. They taught the villagers about AIDS transmission and prevention. Then on Friday, the 5th, 6th and 7th graders had a program designed for their age group. Lots of information was shared and seemed to be well received. In total, over four hundred people attended.

Bwana Kisunga and three nurses slept in my little house that week. Six of my jam making mamas cooked three meals a day for them. It was an exhausting week for me, yet I was elated about the information that was shared and had great hopes for the future of better health in my village. Just the fact that the villagers were now speaking more freely about *ukimwi* (AIDS) meant that progress had been made.

I was reminded of a conversation I had had with a pastor a few months earlier. I had been talking with him about the need for *ukimwi* education and he asked me to stop saying that word so loud. Even a conversation about AIDS was embarrassing. But now, thanks to our week of meetings, people were more comfortable talking about it. And if they could talk about the problem, hopefully, they would do something to alleviate it.

So, we were making progress, but, as is so often the case, change takes time. Of the four hundred people who attended the seminar, only two hundred agreed to get tested. Of those, twenty-six tested positive. I was certain that many of those who didn't get tested were probably afraid of finding out they were positive. There was still work to be done.

HIV/AIDS was such a big problem in Africa, it was considered a pandemic. Now that our villagers had learned about how the disease was transmitted, I hoped there would be a reduction in the number of new cases. Only time would tell.

The last day of the seminar was for the village government evaluation of the program. We also held a closing ceremony. The villagers seemed truly appreciative to the speakers and me for giving them much needed information. They brought us gifts of corn and potatoes throughout the week.

As people began to talk more freely about *ukimwi,* word about our conference spread even to Njombe. Everyone was talking about Bibi Kay's weeklong *ukimwi* seminar. I was hopeful that the stigma surrounding AIDS would be lifted, at least a little.

As the conference ended and things returned to normal, I was happy to see that the villagers were beginning to feel even more comfortable coming to me to talk about it. One day, two women came to my house. They were thirty and forty years old, and now, for the first time, felt they could talk about their disease. Two other women came the next day. Word was spreading.

Another day, a man came to see me privately. He told me he had tested positive. I took him to our HIV Victory Garden, and we cut some Swiss chard and collards. I also gave him some fruit and told him to start eating these types of foods. Good nutrition is so important for those infected with the virus. Villagers practically lived on *ugali,* which had very little nutritional value!

Just as the villagers were starting to come to me for counseling, I was making plans to return to the United States for a few weeks with my family. Before I left, I decided to form a support group to start after my return. I had enough money left in our grant that I could provide speakers for the group every month. I knew that my Swahili wasn't good enough to make me a good counselor, but I could bring in other support. We could meet in the dispensary after it was completed. I would teach nutrition, and we could have discussions. Just one more reason to get that building completed!

CHAPTER TWENTY
Home Sweet Home

In late May, I took a vacation and went back to the United States to visit with my family and friends. I spent time in Arkansas, Missouri and Minnesota. I was only home for two weeks, and the time flew quickly. I didn't get to see all the people I had hoped to, because I ran out of time! I told everyone about my new home in Uhekule and all the friends I had made there. I was excited to share with them about the things we had already accomplished and asked for their prayers and support as we continued.

I told them about some of the people in the village, especially the children. I described ten-year-old Joina who had been through a tragic accident as a toddler. As was the custom, her mother went about doing work and cooking with a baby strapped onto her back. One day Joina's mama was enjoying a little homemade brew while she was working over the open fire. She stumbled and fell. The baby rolled into the cooking fire placing her hands out in front of her to stop the fall. Her little hands were severely burned.

If such a tragedy had happened in the United States, I imagine her hands would have been saved. But in Africa, things are so different. The local doctor told the family that Joina's burns were beyond his ability to treat. He recommended that she be taken to Muhimbili Hospital in Dar, which was hundreds of miles away. The family had no money for such a trip, so they treated her with plant medicine from the forest. I can only imagine the horrible pain that poor baby endured. Eventually, all her fingers fell off.

I told everyone about Joina's only sister Edwina, who was twelve. Edwina was a big help to her handicapped little sister, assisting with dressing and eating and bathing. But Edwina died, apparently of malaria, and now there was no one to help Joina.

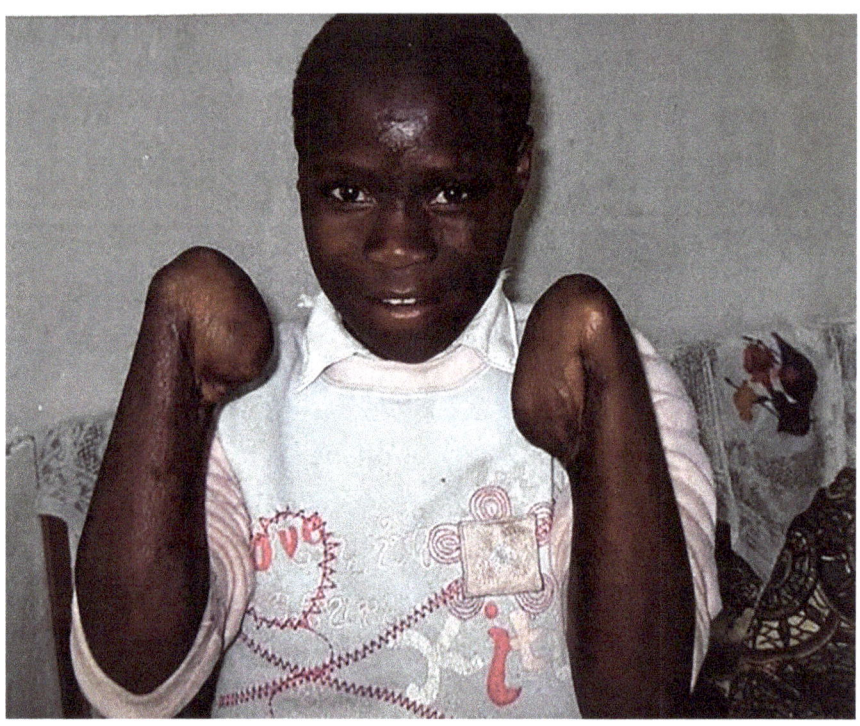

Joina – her hands were burned in a horrific accident – but still she smiles!

I tried to explain to my friends and family about the dire need for proper medical care in Tanzania. I told them about one of the little girls who had injured her arm. Her mama knew something was wrong but was told she needed to take the child to Kibena Hospital in Njombe for x-rays. They could not afford to ride the bus, so the mama borrowed a bicycle, and she rode her four-year-old daughter twenty-four kilometers to town. That poor little girl, with a broken arm, had to cling on to her mother as they bounced along the rough roads. It must have been extremely painful. But pain and discomfort are a part of life in my village.

After it was determined that her arm was broken, she was fitted with a sling and told to return home. So off they went on the bicycle, back to Uhekule. When I heard about this, I was more determined than ever to bring medical help to the village.

I attempted to explain some of the cultural differences I had encountered in Africa. I remembered being surprised when I saw men holding hands and then learned that it was perfectly acceptable and was not suggestive of a sexual relationship. Everyone laughed when I told them about my encounter with Nelson and his friend Martin. When I saw them walking hand in hand and told Nelson that in America, handholding was a sign of a relationship, they immediately dropped hands and emphatically declared that they were not gay.

I told my family about the greetings exchanged between people. When you meet, you take the person's hand and if it is a good friend, you snap your middle finger with theirs three times. That took a bit to get used to! Then the verbal greetings start and go on for several minutes. "How is your home, your family, your parents, your work?" and so on. The villagers are very friendly and want to know all about you. If I was waiting for a bus, they would ask where I was going. And word would spread quickly through the village – gossip was prevalent.

Another cultural difference concerned the discipline of children. Physical punishment was dealt out for even the slightest of misbehavior. I relayed a story I had learned from a PCV from another village. He told me about a young boy named Ezikel. Ezikel was often late to school because his father required him to do chores every morning before he left for class. He began his chores as soon as the sun came up, but never finished in time to get to school on time.

It was a long walk to school, and even though Ezikel ran most of the way, he was consistently late. To encourage him to be on time, his teachers beat Ezikel with a bamboo switch when he arrived late. After weeks and weeks of this treatment, the poor boy couldn't take it anymore. He told his teacher he just wanted to die, but no one took him seriously. Ezikel went home and drank some poison. His cause of death was listed as accidental.

The PCV who told me this story was very shaken up almost to the point of tears. He asked me, "What can we do to stop this punishment? The children are being beaten at school. It isn't right." I had no real answer.

Not all my stories about children were so sad. I also talked about the joy and laughter when I watched the children play football. I told them about the kindergarten children, leaning on my fence, calling for my dog, Shadow, to come and play. My, how those little children cheered when Shadow came running! The memory of their smiles made me smile, too.

Of course, even while I was home, I was thinking about my village. I was most concerned about the HIV positive people, who had no medical care unless they went to Njombe. Sometimes I thought I should call President Carter and complain about the way PEPFAR money is being spent. The funds can be used for antiretroviral medications, but the infected person's blood count must be at a certain level, and monitoring that required visits to trained medical personnel. Getting to doctors and hospitals required a bus ride of almost two hours. Most of the villagers didn't have the three thousand shillings ($2.00) to pay for the bus ride. I wanted to say, "Just give the PEPFAR money to me, and I will make sure it by-passes corruption and gets to where it will do the most good." I wanted to jump on my soap box and give speeches about the 'wrong' ways our tax dollars were being spent. Since I couldn't really do that, I decided to pursue fundraising on my own with anyone who wanted to donate to the cause. Many supporters, joined together, could do much good. And as the saying goes, 'Every little penny counts.'

I enjoyed my time with my family and friends, but my trip back to the United States was also a little disturbing. Maybe that's what is meant by the term 'culture shock.' I looked around at the comfortable homes, abundance of food, and relative ease of life and contrasted it with the lifestyle of my Uhekule friends. Even when I explained about life in the village, I wasn't sure anyone really 'got it.' Unless someone had experienced a life of poverty, could they really understand it? It was easy to say, "Not my problem." And it's true, we all deal with our own issues in life. But most of us don't fight for survival each and every day. It is easy to settle into a comfortable routine and take for granted how blessed we in the United States have been.

So, I was eager to get back to Uhekule, where I was beginning to feel more and more at home. My heart said that's where I belong.

CHAPTER TWENTY-ONE

Home Again, Home Again

Once again, I found myself in Dar es Salaam, heading to Njombe and then on to Uhekule. As usual, the bus ride to the village was bumpy and dusty, but every leg of the journey took me closer to my new friends, many of whom had become practically family. I couldn't wait to see what progress had been made on the dispensary while I was gone. I was also excited to get the *ukimwi* support group going. I remembered all of the support groups Floyd and I had been a part of (AA, Al-Anon, marriage counseling, family counseling, and more) and realized that now I would be on the giving side of the group, instead of participating as a taker. It seemed just one more way my past had prepared me for this new life of mine.

I had time during my journey home to reflect on the things we had accomplished during my first year in Africa. Working with Peace Corps, advances had been made with the dispensary and the HIV/AIDS training. In addition, I thought about the sustainability projects that had been started, as well as the vegetable garden, which would improve the health of the villagers.

Those children! I believed they were the future of Uhekule. I was determined to do more to help them get ahead in the world. Education was the key. I decided that my next grant would be for improvements to the school. Uhekule only had a primary school, kindergarten through seventh grade. There were eight classrooms and all of them were in bad condition. The school was built in the 1970's, and I don't think any improvements had been made since then. Windows were broken, the cement floor had many deep cracks and holes, the walls needed plaster and paint, and the tin roof was the original. There was no library, and for that matter, only a few books. Frank told me that several students had to share one book. Of course, that made learning difficult.

So, my mind was already working out the details for my next Peace Corps grant. It would be for repairs to the school and the construction of a library. I would need to do some fundraising from friends and churches and anyone who was willing to donate.

My arrival back in the village was one of joyful excitement. My house daughter, Shukuru, was waiting for me with a big hug. She had taken good care of my house and my pets, who also seemed glad to see me. Frank and Patricia welcomed me home with a basket of eggs they had gathered from my chickens. It was good to be home.

The walls of the dispensary were up, and the tin roof was on! I wandered through the construction site and marveled at the space. There would be ten rooms and even two showers and two *choo*. And water! The dispensary would be the only building in the village that had running water. There were even six sinks - what a luxury!

I was glad to see that Jerod, (the *fundi* who had built my sit-down toilet), was taking an active role in the construction of the dispensary.

About once a week, I would go to Njombe. I could usually use the internet there (never a guarantee) and I sent monthly newsletters to supporters in the United States. Right away, I started asking for donations for the school and library. I estimated that the cost would be about $15,000, and I encouraged everyone I knew to send tax deductible donations. I hoped to be able to raise the entire amount, either by the grant or through donations. The dispensary project had gone over budget, and I had personally given about $2,000. I didn't want that to happen again, yet I felt strongly that education was important, so I was willing to give what was necessary, if it came to that.

The school project would be my last as a PCV. It was hard to believe, but my time in Uhekule was almost half over. Peace Corps believed strongly in taking care of its volunteers. We had many training courses throughout our term of service. Every time we met together as a group, it was great to be with the younger volunteers. As I learned about the progress of their projects, I caught their vision. It was always exciting to see how these young people were making a difference in their communities.

Every time I took the bus to Njombe, I saw a young boy selling red onions at the bus stand on the weekends. He had an eager smile as he tried to sell his onions to people getting on or off the buses. I got to know him a little bit. His name was Isaiah, and he was ten years old. Sometimes he helped me carry my packages onto the bus. I looked forward to seeing him on every visit to town.

In July, I went to Dar for the one-week Mid-Service Conference. This consisted of medical and dental exams, as well as a mental health check-in. The Peace Corps leaders wanted to see how we were doing, both physically and mentally. Living out in the bush can be stressful in many ways. Disease, difficult living conditions, loneliness and hard work can take a toll on a volunteer's body and spirit. Peace Corps was aware and provided this Mid-Service visit to meet with each of us individually to see how we were doing.

The volunteers in the Environmental group also had several days of meetings dealing with new ways of gardening and water management. This was information I could use in Uhekule.

While in Dar at the conference, I made note of an inspiring quote from Henry Van Dyke. He wrote, "To desire and strive to be of some service to the world, to aim at doing something which shall really increase the happiness and welfare and virtue of mankind… this is a choice which is possible for all of us; and surely it is a good haven to sail for." With that thought fresh in my mind, I returned to Uhekule with a new resolve. We had a lot to do, and only one year left to do it!

CHAPTER TWENTY-TWO

Encounter with a Snake

One day, I was working in my flower gardens in front of my house, down on my hands and knees, pulling weeds and trying to straighten up the flower beds. Suddenly, I disturbed a snake. I think I surprised him as much as he surprised me! He slithered along the wall of the house as I jumped back and yelled for help. "*Siadia, Siadia,*" I called. Soon neighbors came running to see what the matter was. I breathlessly explained I had seen a snake, and the neighbors began to pull apart the whole garden, looking for it. That snake must have been frightened by my frantic yelling, because he was nowhere to be seen. I hoped he had learned to stay away from my house, but I rather expected to see him, or his family, sometime. There are a lot of snakes in Tanzania.

I had invited a neighbor, Fredy Mbilinyi, and his three children to my house for a meal that evening. We sat around my table, and I told them about my encounter with the snake. The children, Margaret, Nuru and Ima, talked to me about snakes they had seen. The oldest girl, Margaret, told me that whenever I saw a snake I should move back and let the snake have space to get away from me. I told her that was good advice, and I would be sure and do that if I ever saw another snake. Margaret said I would surely see more, because there are many around.

After Fredy finished eating, he took his plate out to the *bomba* to rinse, as was the custom. I stayed inside with the children as we finished eating. Suddenly, we heard Fredy calling out "I killed it! It's dead!" We all ran out to see.

Fredy said that Molly, my cat, had been acting strangely. She was jumping up, stalking something, and pouncing. Fredy went to investigate and saw the snake. It seemed to be sick or hurt, he said. It was moving slowly and was easy to kill with a hoe Fredy found leaning against the house.

The snake was dead, so I went to pick it up. Everyone cautioned me not to touch it, but I was curious. I pushed a stick into the snake's mouth and brought down the long fang. This was a viper, very poisonous. I was glad it was no longer a threat to me.

Sometimes snake meat was eaten by the villagers, but we decided to bury this guy.

CHAPTER TWENTY-THREE
A Month of Tears

Care packages were always welcomed while I was in Uhekule. Each delivery was a surprise, and every item was appreciated. One day I was blessed beyond measure when a huge package arrived from my daughter, Jill. Most of the things in the box were for me, but down at the bottom, I found three small gifts for Joina, the little girl who had no hands. I was moved to tears by Jill's thoughtfulness.

I invited Joina to come over to my house to get her gifts. My goodness was that little girl excited. Watching her walk home, her little arms tightly clutching the gifts to her chest, seeing the smile on her face, brought me to tears again. I knew Joina was going to a home with a dirt floor, thatched roof, and pure poverty. But she was going, happy that someone had been so kind. My tears were tears of joy and thankfulness.

The very next day, Joina was knocking on my door. She had made the mile long walk from her home to mine, bringing *me* a thank-you gift. Hooked over the crook of her arm was a small basket of potatoes, a *zawadi* (gift) for me. Knowing that she had very little food at home but was willing to share with me touched my heart. I was grateful and almost (but not quite) cried again.

A week later I really did cry. I had gone to Njombe to do some shopping and meet with the dispensary committee. I also picked up my mail, but I did not open it until I was in my 'hotel' room later that day. There were four envelopes addressed to me and as I opened each one, tears of gratitude flowed down my cheeks. Each envelope contained a check for the school library and renovations. The last check I opened was for $5,000! I couldn't believe my eyes. I was beginning to fear the school/library project would not bring in enough donations to make it feasible, but this wonderful woman gave me hope! I didn't even know the woman who sent that money – she was a friend of one of my friends in Arkansas.

In Tanzania, there is a saying 'If God wishes.' I had received well over half of my goal for donations to the school project, and I believed the rest would come as well, 'if God wishes.'

CHAPTER TWENTY-FOUR
Harvest Time

August in Tanzania is harvest time for wheat and corn. It was a busy season and as usual, most of the work was done by the women. One of the things I noticed when I first arrived in Uhekule was that the women were very hard workers and most of the men treated them more like employees than partners. I've never been afraid of hard work, but I believe in fairness, too! It is another example of cultural differences that will take time to overcome.

The leader of our Lutheran church, Pastor Ngeve, and his family lived about four miles from my home. When he announced to the church that his wife was ill, there was an instant outpouring of compassion. Women made meals for the family and cared for the six children. Shukuru and I cooked potatoes, carrots, peas and beans and took it to them. The pastor's wife was in bed, unable to move because of severe pain in her legs from knee to hip. The pastor's sister also lived in the home, but she was a cripple. Clearly, this family needed some help.

When we arrived, Shukuru did the laundry for the family. With six children, there was a lot to do. I joined a small group of villagers who were breaking rocks. I used a hammer and broke large rocks into smaller pieces and then even smaller bits to make gravel. The gravel would be used in the construction of a new church building.

As more villagers arrived, I left the rock breaking group and joined some women headed to the pastor's wheat field. The first hour there, we cut the wheat by hand using a tool that resembles a small scythe. Then it was laid out to dry.

Part of the field had been cut a few days before and was dry already. We gathered up the dried wheat and carried it to a large mat. The pastor's wife and sister had sewn together heavy plastic bags to make this mat. The wheat was placed on the mat in six rows about twelve feet long.

Shukuru and the pastor's niece cut sticks from a bush-like tree. These sticks were strong and flexible. For the next four hours, the five of us beat the wheat with these sticks. This caused the heads of the wheat to release from the stems.

It was hard work – and I felt it in every muscle of my shoulders, arms and back. Yet the other women kept at it, hour after hour, with no break and no complaint. I had to admire their work ethic and willingness to do all this for the pastor and his family.

The stems of the wheat were removed from the mat and only the grains of wheat and the chaff remained. Then the wheat was thrown up in the air from an *umgo* (woven flat basket) and the wind would blow away the chaff, letting the heavier grains of wheat to fall back onto the *umgo*.

This process depended on wind, and sometimes there was none! As we five women sat on the ground, waiting for the wind to pick up so we could toss the wheat into the air, Pastor Ngeve came to the field to see how the harvest was going. We explained that there wasn't enough wind to finish the job. The pastor told us a story about when he was a little boy. He said he was working in the fields with his mother, and she would 'call the wind.' He proceeded to utter a strange, eerie whistling sound, waving his hands in mesmerizing patterns. It was incredible to watch and listen to. Even more incredible – the wind came! We finished our work, gathered up about a bushel of grain, and headed back to the pastor's house. I knew the picture planted in my mind that day would not soon be forgotten.

Shukuru carried a basket of grain on her head and the pastor fastened a bag of the remaining grain onto his bicycle. I helped Pastor push his bike up the hills and we talked as we walked along. I told him that in America a machine could have done all that work in half an hour, but here it had taken five women five hours to yield a bushel of grain.

I recalled all the acres and acres of farmland in the United States, and the massive inventory of equipment it took to plant and harvest crops and get them to the mills and markets. And here, in Tanzania, there was one old broken-down tractor in our village. What a difference a modern machine or two would have made for these villagers.

We were tired when we finally returned to Uhekule. Shukuru and I were happy to fall into our comfortable beds. Before I fell asleep, however, I prayed for the pastor and his family. I also thought about all the hard work we, and other villagers, had put in today. No wonder Tanzanians in the bush don't live long! If HIV/AIDS doesn't kill them, the hard work of planting, cultivating and harvesting will.

The next morning, it was hard to get out of bed and get going. My early morning chores usually included feeding my chickens between 5:30 and 6:00, but that morning, I was late. When I finally got around to feeding them, the rooster let me know he was not happy with my tardiness. I scattered some grain for the hens, and as usual the rooster stood at the side to let them start eating first. He always did that – which I thought was an admirable quality, and a character trait I would like to see in more of the Tanzanian men. Instead of treating women as second-class citizens, I wished women were considered more as equals.

But that day, the rooster told me in no uncertain terms that I was late with breakfast, and he was not going to tolerate my laziness. He came at me, feathers ruffled, and pecked at my hand, hard enough to draw blood. It was a reminder not to be late again! I couldn't blame him, really. He was just looking after the best interests of his lady friends. Another quality I hoped to see more of in the Tanzanian men!

CHAPTER TWENTY-FIVE
Progress and More Plans

In September, construction on the dispensary was completed and the walls were painted. Ten rooms, two *choos,* two showers and several sinks with running water were ready. Unfortunately, we discovered that there was a problem with the windows. The government inspection of the building declared that the window frames had not been built strong enough to handle the strong wind gusts that hammer Uhekule during the dry season. So, seventy-six window frames had to be replaced. It was a little setback, but we were determined to get the work done correctly and as soon as possible!

Despite the delay caused by the windows, things were coming together nicely with the dispensary. I also had great news about the library grant. My fundraising efforts had paid off, and Peace Corps had received enough donations to enable Uhekule to not only build a library but also one new classroom. There was expected to be some money left over, so the thirty-two-year-old school building could get some minor repairs, too! The school committee met with me and the village government and decided the school building really needed to be replaced, but for now there was only money for some fixups.

More good news came when TASAF, an NGO (Non-Governmental Organization) sent an officer out to Uhekule to look around. When Christina got out of her car, she came up to me and said, "Kay, what did you do here?" I showed her through the library and new classroom, and she was quite impressed.

She looked around at the old section of the school and said, "But look at this part. This is terrible. It should be torn down." I explained that we had done the best we could with the donations we had received, but Christina had a better plan.

"We'll tear this all down and build you a better school," she said. She promised to build three brand new classrooms and a small office. One wing of the old building was left standing, but at least TASAF would fund the new space and oversee its construction.

So, we would be getting a library, four new classrooms, and some repairs on the rest of the building. I could hardly wait to see the school children learning in their new classrooms, reading in the library, and benefiting from the generosity of American supporters they had never even met.

Americans have been blessed to live in a great country, with an excellent education system, advanced medical care, and a multitude of modern conveniences. I was thankful for so many people who had decided to share some of their bounty with Peace Corps and the villagers in Uhekule. Life in a small part of the world would be a little bit better because of the caring gifts from compassionate friends in America.

I decided to work on a couple of smaller projects that could be done without acquiring grant money. These projects would include building and stocking fishponds, raising rabbits for nutrition and income, and teaching my three jam groups how to market their product. In addition, I wanted to enlarge the HIV Victory Garden and get more people involved. These were projects that could be of huge benefit and wouldn't cost too much to get going.

But then I had a new idea. I wanted to take the oldest school students on a field trip to Njombe. These children, seventh graders, had never been to the town. They had never seen a computer; in fact, most of the schoolteachers had never used a computer either.

I had become friends with the owner of the café that had internet connection, so I asked if he would be willing to show the children how a computer works and what it could do. He agreed, so I wrote for a small Peace Corp grant to cover the cost of transportation for the students and their teachers.

I was hoping that we could do the trip to Njombe in the spring. I was thinking that it might motivate the students and possibly more would pass the National Examination that would be held at the end of their seventh year of school.

The school in Uhekule only went to seventh grade. If a student intended to take higher classes, he had to first pass the National Examination. In past years, only about 20% of the children who took the test were able to pass it. If a child is fortunate enough to pass the test, he would be eligible for Form 1 (like junior high school). However, attending this school was very expensive and very few village families could afford it. Primary school was free, but secondary school (Forms 1-4) costs about $1000.00 US dollars a year. That is much more than the villagers can spend, so most of the children stopped their education at the end of seventh grade.

I believed strongly that education was the key to a better life in Uhekule. I recruited seven sponsors (from the United States) who were willing to donate towards the education of some of my village students. It's amazing to think that just $1000 a year will provide an education to African children. So many people in America would hardly miss $1000, but that small amount goes so far in Tanzania. I was thankful for the gifts and hopeful for the good things these students would accomplish in the future.

CHAPTER TWENTY-SIX
Creatures and Corruption

The next few months flew by in a blur, while at the same time, some things were moving slowly. The approval for the library grant took over two months. The people of Uhekule were waiting excitedly for the approval and couldn't wait to see the work starting. But there was nothing we could do to speed up the approval process, so we just had to wait as patiently as possible.

While I was waiting, I took a little vacation. I visited Malawi, a country located south of Tanzania. I traveled with a couple from Njombe in his company Land Cruiser. The car was very old, and it was a twelve hour 'shake, rattle and roll' to our destination. We went to the Majeta Park Preserve to visit with my Peace Corps friend, Sue Borah.

The country of Malawi is very beautiful, especially the drive along Lake Malawi. This lake is the third largest body of water in Africa, separating the countries of Tanzania, Malawi and Mozambique. The Tanzanians call it Lake Nyasa and it boarders the country on the west. The lake is one of the most popular African vacation sites. The views are breathtaking, including mountains with lush green plant life, miles and miles of beaches with golden sand, and brilliant blue waters.

The park preserve was amazing. We saw an abundance of animals including African elephants, leopards, rhinos and monkeys. African buffalo, hippos, warthogs and zebras were there, as well as impala and antelopes. It was an adventure that I never would have experienced had it not been for my involvement with Peace Corps.

We stayed in 'safari tents' on the preserve. The enclosure was very nice – several steps above the normal tent we might envision. There was even a bathroom with a tiled floor! But one day I walked into our fancy tent just in time to see a four-foot viper snake slithering its way around my bed! I left the tent quickly and went to get someone to help me get the viper out of my tent. There was only one person in the lodge – the cook. He came out with a broom and, even though we practically turned the tent upside down, we never did find that snake. I told Sue about it when she returned and her response was, "Well, the snakes were here first, so we are the intruders." I liked that attitude but didn't like the idea of sharing my tent with a viper. Fortunately, I never saw him again – although that doesn't mean he wasn't there!

While in Malawi I had an encounter with government officials – and I think I'd rather meet a viper in my tent! I was taking pictures as we drove along Lake Mawali when we came upon a roadblock. The roads in Africa are often closed for a number of reasons. Sometimes the military police close the roads to impose fines or other restrictions on travelers. You never really know! But this time, apparently the guard didn't like me taking pictures of the military and their government building (which was just a lean-to shack.) He commanded me to step out of the vehicle and proceeded to take my camera away from me. He took me inside the little building and sat opposite me, grilling me with questions. I tried to explain that I was a tourist, and tourists take pictures, but he acted like that was not a satisfactory answer. He said, "This country has lots of problems," as if that explained why I wasn't allowed to take pictures of him. He really didn't like when I answered him, "Yes, I know…corruption being one of them." I was lucky he gave me my camera back and sent me on my way.

When I got back to the car, my friends told me they were very concerned about me and frightened about what was happening to me. I could only imagine what they had been thinking as they waited for my release. If I had been arrested, my friends would have had to call PC in Dar and tell them, "Bibi Kay is in jail in Mawali." I wondered if that had ever happened to a Peace Corps volunteer before.

During our preservice training, and again at Mid-term, volunteers had been instructed about 'Safety and Security.' It was very important to PC staff that we knew how to stay safe in our villages and while traveling. But I don't recall them ever saying it was illegal to take pictures of military policemen and government buildings.

It was interesting to me that I had never felt frightened or worried while in Africa, except this one time when the police were involved. The officers, who should have made me feel safe and protected, were the cause of worry and concern. Even in the remote villages, among strangers, in the dark, I never experienced fear. In fact, I think I was more fearful living in Hot Springs Village, Arkansas, where my home backed up to a wooded area, and I would hear strange noises in the night. I never felt unsafe in Africa, - even the snakes didn't really frighten me! I respected them and tried to give them plenty of space. I didn't fear snakes as much as I feared the unscrupulous officers who sometimes tried to take advantage of people for their own gain.

CHAPTER TWENTY-SEVEN
Reasons to Celebrate

In late October of 2006, I attended a celebration in Dar to commemorate the 45th anniversary of the Peace Corps. Thirty volunteers in Tanzania were there, as well as ten ex-volunteers who had served from 1962-1964. They were mostly nurses who had stayed in groups of eight at Tanzanian hospitals. One of them gave a lovely speech, and I later had time to talk with her. She couldn't believe that I was serving at my age, but my response was, "I could never have done this job at age twenty-two!"

I received a letter from a friend back in the states. She wrote about how hard it would be for me to leave Tanzania when my PC tour was up. She joked about how Africa can 'get in your blood.' Unfortunately, a little bit of Africa did get into my blood – in the form of malaria. It was just a mild case, thanks to the malaria prophylaxis I had taken faithfully. The PC doctor said that it had reduced the effects of the illness drastically. I was only out of commission for three days and then felt fine.

In late November, I took the bus again – another twelve-hour trip from Njombe back to Dar. Peace Corps volunteers had again been invited to the US Ambassador's home for the holiday. This time, the Ambassador was living in a new (even grander) home. The gardens were beautiful, the food delicious and abundant, the wine and beer flowed freely. There was a huge white canopy set up outside, with a live band playing and people dancing on the lawn.

I asked the band leader if they knew any songs from the 50's. They surprised me by playing three songs, one being Mack the Knife. I loved dancing to those songs from the early days of rock and roll. I think I surprised some of the younger PCV's with my dance moves. They thought I was pretty cool!

Before I left Dar, I took our jam around to several other hotels. I was able to secure jam orders from three more hotels. I felt pretty good about that – now the mamas would have some consistent income. Then I went to see the executive chef at the Kilimanjaro Hotel (a five-star hotel equal to any in the US). The head chef was a friend of mine, an Indian who wanted to help the mamas 'in the bush' from my village. He asked me if we could send him 500 jars of jam! I nearly fell over in shock! He told me he wanted to make gift baskets filled with goodies to give away as Christmas gifts.

That was a big order! I bought as many jars as I could find in Dar and for the next two weeks, the mamas worked twelve-hour days making *embe* (mango) jam in my house and courtyard. It was a hectic, chaotic time – and so noisy! The women with little children would bring them along, which added to the confusion and noise. My small house was filled with women, chattering in Swahili, often doing more talking than cooking. I sometimes lost my patience when the women seemed to forget we had lots to do in order to meet our time deadline. Whenever I had to pull their attention to the work yet to be done, they would say, "*Pole sana, Bibi Kay.*" (so very sorry)

And yet the talking, talking, talking continued, and I was getting frustrated. Finally, I told them that when President Kikwete spreads some jam on his *mkate* (bread) and finds an *nzi* (fly) in his jam, he would be very upset. I said "You will be so embarrassed, and the president will never want jam from you again. That will be the end of your jam business." Of course, they laughed, but to press the point, I went on. "The hotel will be sending these gift baskets to all the important people in Parliament and presidents of large companies. You want to be proud of your jam, not embarrassed by *nzi!*" (flies) Then the mamas got really excited and did a better job of paying attention. The talking didn't stop, though!

Two other hotels heard about what we were doing and ordered thirty jars each. We ran out of jars and had to cut their orders in half, and I decided I would need to start collecting jars for next year's busy season. I felt like we could sell as much as we could make. It was turning into a good business. I did wonder how it would continue once I left the village next year. Would the next PCV want to take over this enterprise?

I decided to take a few of the Mamas with me to deliver the jam to the hotels. For most of them, this was their first trip to either Njombe or Dar, and it was a whole new world for them. I watched as their eyes widened when they looked upon high-rise buildings and the opulence in some of the homes. They had never seen so many people and cars and shops and markets. I could just see them gazing around the city in wonder. But when I took them inside the hotel, I almost lost them! We went up in an elevator-and oh my! The shrieks and gasps echoed through the elevator car! White-knuckled and bug-eyed, they held on to me for dear life. It was an experience they would never forget!

Something I wouldn't forget happened when I went into a public restroom in the hotel. I noticed a sign on the wall above each *choo*. It showed a toilet with a silhouette of a person sitting on it. There was another picture with the person standing on the toilet seat and squatting over the hole. That picture had a big red X over it. I had to chuckle – and remember what Floyd said about 'uncivilized natives.' Here was a prime example of how the natives were being taught more civilized ways. They were learning how to properly use a toilet!

While we were in Dar, I took the mamas to see the ocean. There was a look of awe and amazement on their faces as they looked upon the vast expanse of the Indian Ocean. These ladies from the bush, who had never left the vicinity of their village, were seeing things they had never seen before – things they had never even heard of or imagined. An ocean, spreading out as far as they could see, made an impression on them. They lived in a big world but had only experienced one small corner of it. It was a lot to take in.

When we boarded the bus for our return trip to Uhekule, I again saw the boy, Isaiah, who sold onions at the bus stop. He smiled from ear to ear when he recognized me. I bought an onion from him, not because I needed it, but to give him a sale. It wasn't much, but it seemed like a lot to him. These children, and their families, get by on so little.

I had been invited several times to speak at various churches in Uhekule and other nearby villages. I always spoke to them in Swahili, but sometimes it was more successful than others. I knew the more I practiced, the better I would be, so I tried to never turn down the opportunity to speak in front of a large group.

The church in the neighboring village of Ng'anda invited me to go with them on a bus trip to Mhaji, about 40 kilometers away. Their choir was going to be singing at some special services being held there, and they wanted me to go along. So early on a Sunday morning, Shukuru and I crowded onto a small bus and started out on the journey.

The bus ride was joyous! The choir filled the bus with beautiful music. It was a spiritual trip. There is something magical about music that praises God, no matter what the language.

Mhaji was the village where our Lutheran pastor was raised and where he will live when he retires in a few years. At this special church service, there would be lots of music from many choirs and preaching by an evangelist. As a 'special guest,' I was given a seat up front with the evangelist. I was asked to introduce myself and tell a little about why I had come to Tanzania. I spoke from the podium for maybe ten minutes, greeting over 300 people. I can say with confidence that my Swahili flowed flawlessly that day. I didn't stammer or stutter or struggle for the words. I think that day more than any other, I was feeling the spirit of God in the occasion.

The service lasted three hours. The spoken message was good, but the music was fantastic. The choirs sang with no instruments to accompany them except a cow-skin drum. The harmony was heavenly and made background music unnecessary. Joy radiated on the faces of the musicians. It was an experience I wanted to remember forever.

At 1:30, the mamas of the church served food to their guests. They had prepared a feast for us, probably forty people. I was given a huge plate with rice, beans and a vegetable called *mchicha* (like spinach). I sat waiting for a fork or a spoon in order to eat, but I realized that everyone was using their fingers, and no spoon was offered to me. So, I really had no choice but to start eating with my fingers, too. What a mess I made! Of course, everyone was watching me and trying to hold back their laughter. They know Americans use utensils to eat, but I do believe they don't think of me as an American anymore. I'm just like one of them, one of the family. And I can say I also feel that way. I don't see color - we are all the same. Black skin, white skin, young or old – it doesn't matter. What *does* matter is love and respect, and that's what I felt from my friends in Uhekule and other parts of Tanzania.

I appreciated being accepted by the villagers, but I determined that I would carry a *kijiko* (spoon)with me for use on future occasions.

Christmas came to Uhekule and all our hearts were even more joyful than usual. There were, again, no decorations in the village, or presents under a tree, but joy radiated everywhere as people thought about the birth of *Jesu Kristo*. We attended church on Sunday, Christmas Day, and Boxer Day. I spent part of the holiday at my pastor's house in Ng'anda and some of the time with my friends in Uhekule. I thought about other Christmases in the past – how busy and hectic and frazzled I often was as I tried to make everything perfect for my family. But here, now, that seemed so superficial. The important thing was to prepare for Christmas in our hearts, and the villagers had shown me how that's done: with simple joy.

CHAPTER TWENTY-EIGHT
New Year – New Adventures

There was great news at the beginning of 2007 – the dispensary was finished! I believed this building would serve as a small hospital, which was so badly needed in the area. Getting a doctor to serve in Uhekule would be our next task. I had a meeting with Dr. Ruanda, the District Medical Officer in Njombe. He promised that the district would build and pay for a home in Uhekule where the doctor or medical student could live. He informed me that it would be difficult to find a doctor, but a newly graduated medical assistant would be more likely to come and serve the dispensary. I was still hoping for a doctor, if God wishes.

But at least we will have a building - complete with indoor plumbing! It was such a good feeling, knowing I had something to do with the completion of this project. Better still was the knowledge that people in my village and even neighboring villages would soon have access to health care.

At last, the dispensary is complete.

So many people were dying in my village due to the lack of medical services. I continued to attend funerals almost weekly. Sometimes there were several funerals in a week. The hardest of all are the children. My heart breaks for the young lives lost – and often for the sheer lack of medical attention. Whether from TB or AIDS or because of limited prenatal care or an accident, every time there was a funeral for a child, it was so difficult. It seemed like I often witnessed the despair of grief. The Tanzanians have gotten used to it, but I didn't think I ever would.

Aside from the presence of grief, there were things to be joyful about, too. The library and the classrooms were under construction! This was very exciting, not just for me but for the teachers and students as well. In fact, the whole village was happily following the progress.

Because the dispensary took so long to complete, I complained enough to the building committee this time, and work was on track.

I predicted the library would be used by many age groups and for many purposes. Children from the elementary school would have easy access to books for the first time. The nine teachers, some of whom were learning to speak English, would have books in both English and Swahili. Mamas could bring their babies for story time. Secondary students could use the library when they were on school holidays.

I decided to put out a plea to my friends and supporters in the United States. I asked for finances to purchase books, and I also asked for book donations. I suggested the need for story books and picture books in English, which would help with the students learning to speak English. Seventh graders must pass an English section on the National Exam before they can continue to secondary school (grades eight through eleven.) I was helping to teach them, but the books would be an extra reinforcement for what they were learning.

Soon the donations came pouring in. We got deliveries of picture books about animals and plants, geography books with maps, ABC books, Golden Books and more. I also was able to purchase books in Swahili with funds from the grant as well as donations from friends on the other side of the world. There was so much excitement when I returned from Dar bringing crate after crate, each filled with more books! I was very grateful!

So, the library, classroom, and office were being constructed, the supply of books was growing, and my major PC projects were under way. I wasn't done though. There was still more to be accomplished.

I bought two rabbits! And true to form, they had five *watoto* (babies). I had six hutches built for them, and then I bought two

178

more rabbits. We'll fill those hutches in no time! I planned to teach the villagers how to make hutches and raise rabbits. This could provide food and even a profit to their families. It was a small thing and didn't require much investment – but the rewards would be great.

CHAPTER TWENTY-NINE
African Art

About this time, I learned about a local artist who was supposed to be very talented. He was born in the village of Iringa in 1972, and his whole name is Charles Sampson Kiswaga. He started painting at age six, received a certificate in Painting in 2003, and opened a booth at a craft bazaar in Njombe. That's when he shortened his name and became known as Chasaki. I was intrigued by the beautiful work Chasaki did – paintings of village life and nature, scenes, including elephants and other wildlife. I asked if he would do some artwork on the walls of the dispensary.

Before long, Chasaki arrived in Uhekule with his paints and brushes and got to work. I commissioned him to do detailed paintings depicting the development of a fetus. He did a fantastic job of painting the stages of growth in great detail. It was very educational. Of course, very few of the villagers had any understanding of human development before birth, so the paintings drew quite a crowd.

He created two paintings of African animals for me, paintings I will always treasure. I paid him $70 for the two paintings and took them with me the next time I went back to America. Framing for the two large canvases was almost $500! Another example of the inflated costs we experience in the states!

Corrinne and Kay with Chasaki the artist

CHAPTER THIRTY
All is Not Well

My friend, Mike, came to visit me in Uhekule for a month. Unfortunately, we spent most of the time being very ill. In fact, I was running a fever of 104 degrees F, which was worrisome. I somehow managed to get cell service so I could call PC and let them know I was sick. They told me to call for a taxi from Njombe to come pick me up and take me to the hospital. It took the taxi over an hour to reach me in Uhekule, and then another hour ride to the hospital. Because of my past experience at this hospital, I dreaded going. But I had no choice; I was feeling awful.

Being the only *mzungu* (white person) at the hospital, I received lots of attention from the doctors and nurses. However, the amenities at the hospital were sadly lacking. My room had two beds covered with mosquito netting, nothing else. I was so sick the first eight hours, I didn't really care. But then I realized there was no drinking water, and no food offered to me. I had no water for bathing and no toilet paper. It was quite primitive. I finally found a sink and hoped to get drinking water, but the water came out of the faucet looking the color of coffee. I ended up giving a nurse some money and asked her to buy me some drinking water and some toilet paper. The nurses were lovely, the conditions in the hospital were not.

The next morning, four men from Njombe brought me some much-needed relief. Apparently, the taxi driver who transported me to the hospital told them that I was there, and they felt compelled to visit me. These men were originally from Uhekule, so they knew me and wanted to help. They brought me a basin, soap and a gallon of warm water for bathing, as well as some tea and *chapati* (a bread-like food). I appreciated their kindness so very much. Later a married couple came to visit me and gave me 5,000 shillings (about $4.00). At first, I didn't want to accept it, but then I realized it was their custom. Again, I felt the generosity of these African friends.

After thirty hours in the hospital, I was feeling a little better and wanted to get out of there! Peace Corps, always putting the volunteer's health and safety foremost, wanted me to stay in a hotel in town for a few days, to be sure I got enough rest and was fully recovered before I returned to Uhekule. Had I not gotten better, they would have driven from Dar to Njombe to transport me back to a better hospital in Dar. Fortunately, I was able to get back to Uhekule.

Unfortunately, I found Mike sick in bed! He had bronchitis and spent most of his visit feeling miserable. His 'vacation' was not what either of us had hoped. Of the twenty-eight days he was spending in Africa, one or the other of us was sick most of the time.

As I nursed Mike back to health, I was again reminded of the advancements of health care available in the United States. It's so easy to take for granted all the resources Americans have – fresh drinking water and antibiotics, just to name two. What a difference it makes – and most Americans don't even think about it.

I was so grateful for the opportunity to bring a little knowledge to the villagers. Peace Corps was doing wonderful things all around the world, improving the lives of men, women and children in remote villages. I was glad to be a part of it.

But I saw changes in myself, as well. I was now more focused on the needs of others. I was more appreciative of the little things.

I was thankful for my upbringing, my faith, my struggles and yes, even for the most difficult things I had experienced in my life. All these things had worked together to make me who I was – and I found joy in my growth. I felt like shouting *"Ninashukuru sana!"* (I am very grateful!)

CHAPTER THIRTY-ONE
Gifts

A huge care package arrived from Peaceful Grove United Methodist Church in Cottage Grove, Minnesota. Its delivery created quite a stir in the village. I couldn't get over the feeling of thankfulness that overwhelmed me once again. Inside the gigantic box were 530 gift bags for the children of my village! Each white bag had been decorated by the children of the church. Christmas stickers and drawings covered each bag. Someone wrote on the bag if the gift was for a boy or girl and the age it would fit. Each bag contained school supplies, toys, candy and playdough – gifts from the children in Minnesota to the children of Uhekule.

The excitement among the village children was evident, as was a bit of confusion. These children had never received presents before and didn't even know what to do with the toys and playdough! I had so much fun showing them how to mold the playdough into animals and shapes. My children (yes, I was starting to think of them as 'mine') were thrilled to have toys of their own to play with – a whole new experience for them. They would never forget the experience of receiving a *zawadi* (gift) from American friends.

I will not forget the kind people of my church in Minnesota. It took a lot of planning and organization to get these gift bags to my children in Uhekule. Although the care package was shipped off in plenty of time to get to us by Christmas, it didn't arrive until April. (The Tanzanian postal service leaves a little to be desired.)

But it didn't really matter when the package arrived. The children were completely thrilled.

About that same time, I received a thrill of my own. I was contacted by a man named Paul Maloney. I did not know this man, but somehow, he had been given information about me. I believe a mutual friend of ours had been sharing my monthly newsletters with him. That is how he learned about my work in Uhekule.

Sometimes just the right people feel just the right push at just the right time (call it divine intervention, if you will) and miracles begin to happen. Paul Maloney was certainly feeling a push to assist in making a miracle!

It just so happened that Mr. Maloney owned a silicone factory in Silicon Valley in California. He contacted me, offering to provide solar power to the dispensary in Uhekule. Talk about shock….! I couldn't believe his generosity. To imagine electric power in the dispensary building – well, that was far beyond my biggest dreams!

There are many thoughtful and generous people in the world. I was so thankful for everyone who had given even just a few dollars to help the people of my village. Whether toys in a gift bag, books for the library, a doll for a sick child, or electric power, every gift was appreciated. I was even thankful for the person who had shared my newsletters with Mr. Maloney. That small act had led to an amazing gift. Life in Uhekule was looking a little brighter, and the future for my friends here had a hope that was growing daily. Good things lay ahead, and they were coming due in large part to the caring and compassion of Americans who saw beyond themselves. Kind people who knew the importance of helping others were making a difference in the world.

To think that this man, who I didn't know, was compelled to help people in my distant village, whom he had never met. *Mungu*

(God) continues to shine his light on my work here in Uhekule and *"Ninashukuru sana!"* (I am very grateful.) I was saying that every day!

While I was thinking thankful thoughts, I was also considering the reach of Peace Corps to other parts of the world. I was directly involved with helping the people of Tanzania, but I knew that good work was being done globally as well. Peace Corps was making a difference in the lives of thousands of people. I was so glad to be a part of it – and so grateful for others everywhere who were doing what they could to help those less fortunate than themselves. Miracles were happening all around the world.

In the midst of the excitement about the solar power gift, I realized that the process was going to take quite some time. There was a lot of governmental red tape to get through, as well as shipping times and transportation. The installation of the equipment would be a long time down the road – and I wondered if I would still be in Uhekule to see it all come together. My term of service would be over in four months, unless I extended. I needed to give that some serious thought.

CHAPTER THIRTY-TWO
Peace Corps Public Relations

Another American man got word to me that he would like to meet me. His name was David Monday, and he was an executive at Wachovia Securities. He was planning a trip for a safari in the Serengeti. He had heard about me from a friend of his, Ron Tschetter, who just happened to be the Director of Peace Corps. David was doing research for a book he planned to title "Rockin' in Retirement." It would be a book about options for older, retired people who don't want to sit home watching television or playing solitaire for the rest of their lives.

David came to meet me in Uhekule, and we talked for hours. He is a very interesting man, charismatic and caring in his own way, and he wanted to know all about my work with the villagers. I believe his book will also be a useful tool for Peace Corps, to help recruit other older volunteers. After all, just because a person is retirement age, it doesn't mean his or her usefulness has come to an end. I was proof of that.

.

The following was written by David Monday for inclusion in his book. It is used here with his permission.

Chapter Three
Half a World Away: The Peace Corps
1

Americans, almost by nature, are generous. We respond to calls of need. We support churches, charities, causes, schools, and the list goes on. Many of us give not only because we are moved by the cause, but also because we know how lucky we are to live where water is pure, food is plentiful, travel is safe, medicine is available, our climate is controlled and all of the information in the world is at our fingertips. It's a cliche but it's true; *It doesn't get any better than this!*

Recently I spent some time with an old friend, Ron Tschetter. Ron is the type of friend that makes you think. Conversations with him often end up focused on helping others. Ron is generous, not just with his treasures but with himself. He compounds the effects of his generosity by challenging those around him to give of themselves as well. Ron had just accepted a huge new challenge and now as a result would be challenging an entire generation.

I first met him twenty years ago at a business convention. We quickly became friends, often visiting each other, swapping ideas and war stories. I always enjoyed our conversations, because Ron is upbeat, thoughtful and very experienced, not just in business but in life. He talked often about his stint in the Peace Corps following college. His service had made a huge impact on him and had served to shape much of his character. It was as a Peace Corp volunteer in India, that he fell in love with his wife, and developed his taste for curry.

After his Peace Corps service, Ron moved back home to Minneapolis, succeeded in business, raised a family, retired to Florida, and then, unhappy with the empty stretches of time, went back to work. I guess you would say that he *retired from retirement*. A while ago, serendipity led me to call Ron, and he finally got back to me weeks later. (I was a little concerned because in the past Ron had promptly returned my calls.) "Hi David," he said. "Sorry I couldn't get to you sooner. I've been really busy. The President has just nominated me for *Director of the Peace Corps.*" For Ron, this was a dream come true, a chance to complete his working life back where he began, serving others.

A few weeks later, the United States Senate confirmed the nomination 99-0. I went to Washington for his swearing-in and was moved by the look of firm determination on my old friend's face, moved by the way our eyes linked, and locked, moved mostly by the idea that suddenly sprang to mind; *What a great opportunity for seniors!* Research goes on and on about the effect peer pressure has on adolescents; well, take a look at us too. If he could walk the halls of marble-floored Washington D.C., then why couldn't we walk the dirt paths of some small place far from here? Would that be possible at the age of 50, 60 or 70? Was there a special program for those carrying a hanging bag instead of a backpack? How long is the tour of duty? Can couples go? (Going anywhere for more than a month without my wife is a non-starter for me; I like being with her too much.) Is it safe? What about medical care? And most importantly, *does it make a difference?*

It does. Since JFK established the corps in 1961, over 180,000 people have served throughout the world. Projects are in the areas of education, health, business development, environment, agriculture, and youth. So, no matter what your area of expertise or interest is, there is likely a way for you to make a contribution. You are not required to speak a foreign language, although those with knowledge of French or Spanish are in high demand and will likely have the most choices with respect to their service.

Volunteers, no matter their age, are assigned to a project in one of the 75 countries the corps serves. You must be in reasonably good health because medical care may be scant. Although not a requirement, the vast majority of volunteers had a college degree. The average age of volunteers is 28 (this number will most likely be heading up) and the oldest volunteer is 79. About one tenth of the volunteers are married. There's no paycheck, per se, but you are provided modest housing, food, medical and dental care. Upon completion of your tour of duty you are given a $6,000 reentry stipend. You may also take occasional leaves to return home, at your own expense.

If you are like me, as you get older you are a bit more cautious; we've seen the effects of recklessness that are often associated with youth. So, you're probably wondering about the risk of Peace Corp service. Obviously, spending time in the developing world involves risk. The organization clearly takes its safety responsibilities very seriously. They also publish year by year, country by country, crime statistics. There are wide differences between the various areas served by volunteers. But overall, in any given year there's about a 3% chance of being assaulted (most assaults are minor) and about a 13% chance of being the victim of a crime against property. You'll have to decide if these seem like small numbers or big numbers to you. But once again, your safety really depends on where you serve and the judgement you use (mostly it's just common sense.)

I don't know if I would actually pack up my brand-new duffel bag, put on a cool cap, and haul my wife on Air Mongolia to the outer edges of the earth. For one, I'm not sure she'd be game. For another, I'm not sure I could in fact leave my friends and family and my creature comforts behind for 27 months, which is the required term of service. But that's the nice thing about today's generation of seniors; we come in many shapes, sizes, flavors and varieties. Some of us are singers while others are dancers. We're all different, but our collective numbers are huge. If only one tenth of one percent of those over 50 signed on with the Peace Corps, that would be 10,000 additional ambassadors spreading American kindness, know-how and generosity across the developing world.

Just imagine the impact we could make. And it's not just our numbers. At 50, 60, or even 70, we know a lot more than we did at 20. We've learned important lessons about human nature, about hope and hopelessness, about faith, and about what really matters in life. We might not have the muscle power of a twenty-year-old (truth is, I never had much muscle power), but we often have staying power, patience, wisdom and resolve. In approaching projects, even Peace Corps projects, those who have traveled around the block once or twice have advantages; we know when to stay on course or when to make a change, we understand that family is the universal motivator, and we've learned that very little can be accomplished on our own.

Although the Peace Corps is about helping others and promoting understanding between cultures, I see Peace Corps service as also about the *soul;* not the soul of those served but the soul of the server. Millions of people around the globe risk injury, death, and incarceration just for a chance to live as Americans. The most sought-after cards in the world are the Green Card and the Social Security Card. For most of us, the circumstances of our birth in America is akin to winning the world's biggest jackpot.

The problem is that as we go through our daily lives, working, relaxing, watching TV, and reading, it's easy to forget that 840 million people are hungry, over 100 million are homeless and that most will never taste any of the luxury we too often take for granted. I know we know this; but the problem is we don't often get to feel it. To give up the American life (even for 27 months) and walk in the shoes of the world's most unfortunate people would surely help us avoid the sin of pride, soften our hearts, adjust our prospective. What an opportunity!

Kay Oursler
Bibi to a Village
2

Just visiting a Peace Corps volunteer can be an adventure. I must confess that before my trek, I probably couldn't come close to pointing out Tanzania, home to the Serengeti, on a blank map of Africa. Fly 8 hours from Washington to Amsterdam, change planes and head south another 9 hours, and you'll be in Dar es Salaam, Tanzania's largest city, home to 4 million people, about a tenth of the country's population.

After a night's rest in the luxurious Royal Palm Hotel, I met my driver in the lobby at 7:30 sharp. "We need to leave right away, it's at least a 12 hour drive to the village," said Salmini, my 35 year old Muslim driver. Tanzania is about evenly split between Muslims and Christians. These very different faiths live in relative harmony, partly because of laws preventing speaking ill of any religion in public. A concept that sounds odd to Americans (free speech and all) but which seems to serve Tanzanians fairly well.

The drive was memorable to say the least.

Everything was smooth at first as we headed for the country's remote southern highlands. The road was excellent, easily supporting our 130 kilometer speed (about 80 miles per hour). But about 1 a.m., the situation quickly changed as we found ourselves still speeding along at a good clip, but now dodging some humongous potholes (we're talking three feet wide and a foot deep…the type that could flip you right over), trucks coming head on (they're dodging the potholes as well), bicycles, and people, lots of people – all ages, even 3 year olds walking unescorted on the side of the road. "Don't worry," Salmini said, noting my near rigor mortis as I was stuck to my *left* seat 'shotgun' position. British driving rules apply.

After eleven heart stopping, spine pounding hours, we neared Njombe, a town of about 10,000 where we were to meet our host for the next few days, Kay Oursler, or as the Tanzanians call her, *Bibi Kay.* - more about her later. She would be easy to spot. "I'll be the white face." Just as promised, there she was waving us down with three African orphans at her side. "How was the ride?" she giggles. No sooner had the word 'bumpy' left me when she said, "You haven't seen anything yet. It's another hour to the village, so we must hurry to beat the dark." Kay and her entourage hopped in, and we were off.

It's not easy to size up this lady. Why would a 67-year-old, retired career woman, leave America, including 2 children and 8 grandchildren, travel halfway around the world to live in conditions that even the most unfortunate Americans would call 'primitive? As we made our way toward Uhekule, I began to get a glimpse of what drives this very special woman. "You are going to love the villagers," she said as we crept along the mountain *'road.'* Webster defines road as *'a way made for traveling between two places,'* so I guess this steep washed out path qualifies but trust me here; this road is like none you've ever seen.

As we neared the village, hands began waving and kids were running alongside the car screaming, *"Bibi, Bibi."* Bibi Kay was back and with visitors. Excitement filled the air…excitement and *relief.* Over the next two days, I would understand why.

In many ways, Kay Oursler seems like a normal American. She was married for 46 years, raised 2 children while working in several professional and management jobs as she and her husband moved about the country following his job. Cities like Chicago, Baltimore and Minneapolis were all home to her at points along the way. Her children grew up and made their own families. Kay divorced, retired, and bought a condo in a Hot Springs, Arkansas seniors' community. But here's where the portrait of normalcy begins to blur.

At age 64, heading home from running some errands, Kay approached the scene of a house fire. A young mother stood in the yard crying hysterically as everything she owned smoldered. Kay drove right by without stopping. Most of us are conditioned to do so, telling ourselves that we need to stay out of the way. Let the professionals do the work. We assure ourselves that a loving family is probably nearby, ready to console their mother, brother, sister child….

But, as Kay passed by, she didn't even slow down; she sped up, almost racing home. Flying in the door, she went straight to her desk where she kept her stash of emergency cash. This was certainly an emergency. She headed back to the scene, hugged the young woman and later took her shopping for the essentials that would get this terrified young mother and her family through the next few days. Kay Oursler is a woman of action. (This story was given to David by Mike Moriarty.)

As she settled into retired life, Kay began to reflect on her 60 plus years of living. She had accomplished a lot. She had been successful in her work. The job of raising kids had been a challenge, particularly the teenage years, but everything eventually worked out, and now she was watching her kids face some of the same challenges as they raised their own kids. She had accumulated enough money to be comfortable and owned her share of material possessions. She was also proud that she had managed to remain friendly with her ex-husband.

But, as Kay Oursler worked on making her transition, she had trouble finding *peace.* We all yearn for a time of peace in our lives. As we approach retirement, we naturally think of a period free from the pressures and worries we faced in our younger days. This was very hard for Kay. Her mind kept racing. There were too many loose ends in her life, too much unfinished business. She seemed to have a *calling* to do more, to make more of a difference, to take some risks. Ignoring the stereotypes about her age and the warnings of friends and family, Kay answered her *call* by joining the Peace Corps. She would man an outpost in Uhekule, Tanzania.

Uhekule is severely lacking in many of the creature comforts westerners take for granted. There is no running water, no electricity, and no motor vehicles. The 400 children attend a decrepit primary school with dirt floors, where there is less than one book for every ten students. Although the villagers are among the world's poorest, they are rich in spirit, optimism, and kindness. Deeply religious, 80% attend one of the five churches serving about 500 families. With the odds stacked against them big time, these people press on, working from sunup to sundown tending their crops, caring for and encouraging their children, and helping each other. It's easy to see how they have won the heart of Bibi Kay.

To say that she has assimilated into Uhekule life misses the mark by a mile. In the 18 months she has lived with and among the people of this remote outpost, Bibi Kay has become a human cornerstone of the Community. 'Bibi', by the way, is the Swahili word for 'grandmother.'

She is a friend to everyone. But, more importantly she is also a source of trusted advice…. a *Bibi*… not because of her age, or generations of descendants, but because Bibis around the world are special people. They love us, they see the good in us, they overlook our faults and when we need advice, they provide wisdom. They've learned through trial and error, mistakes and successes, and thousands of observations. Their sight may fail but their vision remains keen.

Kay Oursler is not only Bibi to hundreds of villagers, but to the village itself. She provides counsel, know-how, encouragement, and inspiration. Bibi Kay is a mover and a shaker. She can make things happen. She also doesn't mind giving you a piece of her mind when she knows you can do better. I saw her do this several times. She chastised a woman's group she had organized into a jam making business selling to hotels hundreds of miles away at the coast. They had spent too much of their earnings, leaving the business without enough cash to buy jars for the next batch. The women had been irresponsible, and she let them know she was disappointed.

Her official duties include coordinating several projects, some simple, others more elaborate. She bought two rabbits and is breeding them so that the school children can have a source of protein in their lunch. Today the kids are served a yucky white paste called *ugali*, made of corn flour and water, cooked over an open fire. That's it… the same every day. Thanks to Bibi Kay, the children will soon have meat, at least on some days.

She organized a collective garden where vegetables are raised to feed the sick (most are victims of malaria and AIDS). The village council provided the land, and everyone helps tend the plot. On a grander scale, Bibi Kay helped raise the necessary funds (through the Peace Corp grant process) and coordinated the building of a ten-room dispensary. This first-class structure is now the pride of the village. She's now negotiating with the Minister of Health to provide a doctor.

While she juggles all of this, you may also find her teaching an English class or coordinating HIV awareness seminars. From sunup to sundown, Bibi Kay is on the move. "The villagers need me, and I love them," Bibi says to me several times during our visit. "I'm not sure I can leave them when my term is up."

As I prepared to leave Uhekule, the village officials gave me a letter entitled "The Uhekule Village Report to David." The report listed the many accomplishments of this most extraordinary woman and offers "thanks to all the Americans to send this woman to us. We wish her to live with us for a long time, but the period is limited." As a teary village official handed me the letter he whispered, *"She is our only hope."*

As Salmini and I packed our vehicle for the ride back to the airport in Dar, I spent a few last moments with Bibi Kay. She had headed off to Africa because she wanted to make a difference and find peace. Now nearing the end of her term, peace still eludes her. "I just can't decide. The village needs me, I'm famous here. I'm sure the Peace Corps would accept me for a second term, another year. I could do so much. On the other hand, I really miss my family and the people back home. My boyfriend wants to marry me when I get back. But back at home, I'll just be a *nobody* again."

Bibi Kay is torn. She's the type of person that may always struggle with her *calling*. I hope that one day she will come to understand that although there will always be more to do, more people to help, more adventures to enjoy, she has touched hundreds with her work and thousands through her example. Her ability to love and help people comes not from where she is but from the spirit that lives within her soul. Whether she comes home, or stays in Africa forevermore, Kay Oursler shall carry not only the name but the grand title of *Bibi*.

Getting Started
3

The first step in evaluating Peace Corps service is to ask yourself if you are in a position, physically, emotionally, and financially, to pack your bags and head off for 27 months. While there are 48 days of 'vacation,' most volunteers do not come home during their term of service. You'll need to consider your children, grandchildren, pets, parents and others that may depend on you. Although your first thought may be to consider only the negative effects of your absence, consider also the positive example you would set by embracing such an adventure.

Next, learn the basics. The Peace Corps web site, www.peacecorps. gov is fantastic. It has everything you could possibly want to know. After studying the information, if you are still game, call one of the recruiters, who are located in 13 offices across the country. The phone numbers are on the site. The recruiters will put you in touch with alumni who will be anxious to share their experiences with you. You should talk to several people and in particular seek out those who served where you may be seeking assignment.

Finally, you must apply. You will submit complete background information which includes your work experience, education and many personal details. You will also have to undergo a thorough medical evaluation. If you have medical conditions that might prevent service, you should discuss these upfront with the recruiter to avoid wasted time and disappointment.

The entire process takes six to nine months between the time you apply and the time you step on the plane headed for a place that is likely to be 180 degrees different from where you are now. Upon arrival in your host country, you'll train for about three months with the professional staff in that country. Training will include language, customs, safety and country culture. Then you're off to your project for the next 24 months. Off to new friendships, a new way of living, a new life of service, and most certainly a new perspective!

* * * * *

Although David Monday's book was never published, I still appreciated the time he spent with me. The concept of retirees offering their skills and knowledge to enable under-served countries to advance their citizens is an inspiration. I was glad to, in some way, encourage older adults to get involved with Peace Corps. It's never too late to offer good to the world.

CHAPTER THIRTY-THREE
Growing Things

Thanks to the generosity of so many people and organizations in the United States, my work in Uhekule was moving forward. Every day I said prayers of thanksgiving for the donations and support from so many of my friends and family, and even people I didn't personally know. Americans are the most generous people in the world, and I was so pleased and proud for all the ways my work was being supported. I believed that our 'higher power' was working overtime in Uhekule, and touching hearts there and in the United States. I knew I could never say thank you enough!

Some people in Minnesota and others in Arkansas had expressed an interest in helping with higher education for some of the students who had the desire to go to school beyond the seventh grade. I was able to arrange sponsorship for several children in this way. On an average, I had two or three students (mostly orphans) come and talk with me every month. They told me they want to go to secondary school, but their families can't afford the tuition and boarding costs. My American friends, who sponsor students in primary school, send just $200 a year, and expenses are covered. Costs for secondary school and University are higher, but still average only $2000 a year. It seems like so little to give, but it goes so far here. What I would give for more sponsors. So much more could be done, if only more people were aware of the opportunities and had the heart to help.

My time at Uhekule was drawing to a close. I only had a few months left to wrap up the Peace Corps projects and put finishing touches on plans for sustainability. Some things were easier than others.

The rabbits were growing, and more rabbits were being born. (That was working out just as I had hoped!) I was teaching the mamas how to build pens and raise rabbits for their families. The children would have rabbit meat to add some protein to their diet, at least occasionally.

As a follow-up to the HIV/AIDS training we had held, I was supposed to write a report. I held a meeting to find out how the committees on 'home-based care' and 'peer education support' were doing. I was disappointed to learn that neither of these committees were very active. I thought things had been going better – a few people had been coming to me to talk about their illness, so I thought they were also getting help from the committee members. That turned out to not be the case.

The chairman of the committee told me he knew of twenty-six HIV positive people who were still not willing to talk about their illness. I told him I understand, because there is a stigma attached to the disease. HIV positive people are treated as if they have leprosy.

The Victory Garden was growing, but still not many people participated. Even though the garden was primarily for the sick of the village, usually only a few people came to work with me. I tended the crops every Wednesday, weeding, transplanting, fertilizing, and harvesting. Usually only my HIV positive neighbor came to help me.

One day, as my neighbor friend and I left my home and headed over to the garden, I was pleasantly surprised to see ten mamas coming into my yard. They carried buckets of compost on their heads and were ready to help with the gardening. I almost burst into tears – this was probably the most important event in my service as a PCV. These ten mamas were willing to admit to their positive HIV condition, and were stepping forward, acknowledging to everyone that they were no longer hiding the illness, but were instead seeking help. It was such a big step toward progress! To have these ten mamas come forward was a real blessing to me.

Shukuru fixed a large, wonderful salad of lettuce, carrots, onions, garlic and cucumbers from the garden. She added avocado and cheese and served it with bread and tea. It was a wonderful feast, and everyone had their fill of healthy food. I hoped the mamas would continue to seek out nutritious vegetables and their health would improve. The Victory Garden was going to make a difference in the lives of many.

By April, the library and classroom were nearing completion. Plastering of the walls and plywood for the ceiling was almost finished. Next the walls would be painted. Then the rooms would be set up and could be used by the children. Oh, they were quite excited. (And so was I!) Deliveries of books were coming in one by one, sent from my friends in Minnesota and Arkansas. I had already received about forty books, plus I had financial donations to buy books in Swahili. This library was going to be 'state of the art' – at least by Tanzanian standards. It had already become the envy of other villages, and it wasn't finished yet!

Although progress was moving along at a decent pace (for Tanzania, anway!) I wondered if I would be around to see the final product. Would I see the children using the library, learning English from a donated book? Would I be there when the students got to move into the new classrooms? I only had a few months until my term would be over, and I'd have to leave my village. Could I do it? Could I leave my friends and the children I'd come to love?

I decided to extend my tour with Peace Corps for another six months. There was still so much to do!

CHAPTER THIRTY-FOUR
Green Eyed Monster

Jealousy is a terrible thing. And I saw it raise its ugly head time after time in Tanzania. One day I learned how jealousy can turn to rage and violence. I heard about a man in Njombe who found his wife in bed with a neighbor. His anger boiled to rage, and he took a knife to the offender's genitals. As the man lay on the hospital bed, bleeding and moaning in pain, no medical assistance was given. The doctor had to wait for the police to come and assess the situation. Before long, the man bled to death.

It seemed like there was much resentment aimed at villagers that were improving themselves, or anyone who seemed to be granted favor from the government. Sometimes even the perception of favoritism would lead to anger or resentment.

Gossip is just as bad. One day, my jam mamas told me that they all wanted to be in the group, and they never wanted to miss a day. At first, I was flattered and impressed by their work ethic, but then I came to realize that the real reason no one wanted to be absent was because, if one woman was gone, all the rest would talk about her. The only way to prevent being the subject of gossip was to be there!

For some reason that I didn't understand, villagers started to be suspicious of my friendship with Frank, the headmaster of the primary school and my counterpart. I think some of the government leaders feared the two of us were gaining too much respect and power. The village government made life difficult for Frank and his family, and they decided to leave Uhekule and move to a different school.

Frank's leaving made me sad; he and Patricia had become very good friends of mine, and I would miss them terribly. But I did understand that Frank needed to do what was best for his family. We promised to keep in touch with each other and said goodbye with hugs and tears.

Soon, our school had a new headmaster. His name was Henry, and he moved right into Frank's old house. It was a perk of being a headmaster or a teacher – housing was provided. Henry became my new counterpart.

Corruption was evident throughout the country, and I encountered it from time to time as well. Many times, people in power would create rules and force tariffs on unsuspecting travelers. There might suddenly be a tax on a road or a bridge, and officers would stop vehicles to collect the fee. Usually, the money went right into the officer's own pocket.

Before long, it became known that I would not tolerate unfair treatment. If police officers noticed that I was in the vehicle, they would usually let us pass by unbothered. They knew that I would be upset with them, and they didn't think it was worth it! One time, a village man named Nedkia was going to town and asked me to go along with him. He said if I was in the truck with him, they would not be stopped and questioned or fined. I agreed to travel along, not knowing the real reason behind his trip. It turned out that Nedkia was going to buy a pig, and he knew he would be taxed highly if the police saw it in the truck. But if I was there, they would let him go on without inspection. So, I spent the whole ride home scrunched into the passenger seat with a smelly pig at my feet.

I had learned a lot about injustices in this culture – the inequality of men and women, wealth verses extreme poverty, the sometimes-misused power of governmental officials, and the need for affordable medical care and education for all. I couldn't fix everything but was determined to help whenever and however I could.

CHAPTER THIRTY-FIVE
An Unexpected Blessing

May (2007) arrived in Uhekule and with it came the dust. From December through February, we had rain almost every day. March and April would have rain now and then. But starting on May 1, like clockwork, the rain stopped. We probably wouldn't see rain again until December. Before long, everything was covered with brownish dust. Even the green trees turned brown because the leaves were covered. I didn't see how any living plant could survive, covered like that, but somehow, they always did. The morning glories that grew over my shed were no longer beautiful pink or blue flowers – they were brown. Dust was everywhere. I wiped off my table and five minutes later I needed to do it again.

Temperatures began to drop, too. Our winter was coming. Many mornings I woke up cold, because it was just a few degrees above freezing. I put an extra blanket on the bed – and sometimes two. The sun warmed things to a comfortable temperature by mid-morning and the rest of the day would be quite pleasant. To tell the truth, I loved the climate in Uhekule. It was never too hot, even in the summer. Some winter nights were cold, but I would rather be cold than hot, so that's perfect for me. And just when I felt like I couldn't stand the dust one day longer, the summer rains began. It was a cycle I was beginning to get used to.

I was blessed to receive a letter from Peaceful Grove United Methodist Church in Cottage Grove, Minnesota. They told me of their plans to hold a benefit dinner for 'Kay's Kids.' Of course, I thought that was such a wonderful, thoughtful idea. That church has really gone above and beyond to support me. They have sponsored several students to secondary school, and now this fundraising event was an extra nice gift. I could never thank them enough.

But when their donation arrived, I was totally flabbergasted! The check was for over $1,300. I never dreamed it might be that much; I was thinking probably two or three hundred. I emailed the congregation to ask how they would like the money spent and gave them several options, but they replied that I could use the money however I saw fit.

One obvious need was for new sweaters for the primary school children. The green sweaters required for the school uniforms were all in tatters and rags. They were hardly suitable for the cold mornings we were having. Most of the sweaters had been handed down through many family members and were so worn out, they were practically useless for warmth, not to mention how sad looking they were.

Boys and girls in tattered school sweaters

I went to Njombe and found some women who would make sweaters for the pupils in grades 1-6. Since the 7th graders would be leaving school soon, the new headmaster, Henry, and I decided not to get them sweaters. In total, 352 sweaters were made.

Imagine my amazement when I picked up the sweaters and paid for them, the amount of money I needed was exactly the amount that had been sent by the church in Minnesota. I marveled again at how God was continuing to work in Uhekule. Thanks to these gifts, my children in Uhekule were being clothed.

When I brought the sweaters back to Uhekule, I had a heated discussion with Henry, the headmaster. In typical Tanzanian style, Henry felt that the boys should be fitted for their sweaters first, and the girls would take the leftovers. I put my foot down and insisted that it be done my way: girls first! He didn't like it, but I stood my ground and Henry finally gave in. I was doing what I could to change the attitude of African men! It was time to show the women and girls a little respect!

The children were so happy to be wearing better-looking sweaters. Just having decent clothes can make a difference in a student's enjoyment of school. And knowing that someone cared enough about them to donate the money for the sweaters gave us all a warm, happy feeling. The smiles on those little faces were a sight to behold!

New sweaters and big smiles

The children in Uhekule are raised speaking the tribal language, Kibena. When they start school, the lessons in Swahili begin, although many of them learn some Swahili before going to school. Once they get to standard (grade) six, they begin learning English. The goal is to pass the English section on the National Exam which is given in September of seventh grade. The problem is, most of the teachers in primary school know very little English. That's why I decided to help.

I continued to teach English to the seventh graders, sometimes at school and sometimes at my home after school. As seventh graders, they are expected to know some English, but no one is allowed into secondary school (grades 8-11) unless they pass the English section. For some children, whose hopes of attending secondary school were dashed because of the expense, learning English didn't seem necessary. I tried to convince them that English could help them in many ways, one being that they could communicate better with me!

I thought back to my high school English teacher, Mrs. Webking, and was thankful I had been a good student. What I had learned from her about nouns and verbs, adverbs and adjectives, etc. was coming in handy now, years later.

One day, my house daughter, Shukuru, was sick and could not come help with my cooking and housework. One of the seventh-grade girls came to help me instead. As we were talking, using some English, I was petting my cat, Molly. The girl looked at me strangely and proceeded to tell me that in her sub-village, people eat cats. I hugged Molly a little closer, hoping that the girl wasn't making plans for supper.

Hunger is all around me. Illness, lack of an adequate diet, poor medical conditions are a way of life here. I prayed every day that I could bring a little light into their situation, bring a little hope for a future that wasn't quite so desperate.

I rode my bike almost every day, visiting families in the six sub-villages, doing various chores and keeping up with the progress of all my projects. One day as I was riding, I hit an extra-rough patch on the path and took a spill. I had a two-inch gash on my leg. I limped my way back home and got my first aid kit, including steri-strips to close the gap. Even though I thought it would be fine, the teachers at the school insisted that someone take me to the hospital in Njombe. I didn't want to go, considering my previous stays in that place, but they took me anyway. I returned home with six stitches.

On my way back from Njombe, I took a bus, of course. And as usual, I had a chance to talk with Isaiah, the onion boy. I asked how he was doing, and he said he was just fine. His smile is so contagious.

As usual, the bus was crowded. I shared a seat with a lady I didn't know. She had a baby on her back, a basket in one hand and a *kuku* (chicken) in the other. The chicken ended up on the floor under my feet, which meant I had to grab it for her when she exited the bus. I often feel sorry for these mamas in Tanzania. They always seem to have a baby in tow, walking barefoot through the fields to cultivate their little patch of farmland with just a primitive hoe. It could be said, "The women work hard, and the men hardly work." That's not totally true, but generally speaking, men just give orders and women do the work. They feel like men are superior and women must take second place.

One day I was in Njombe at a *soko* (market) buying rice. A man came up to the shopkeeper and started to order. He saw that I was there, yet he jumped right ahead of me. I said with a scowl *"Samahani lakini mimi ni wa kwanza."* ("Excuse me! But I'm first!") I won't put up with the pompous attitudes of some men. It's rather shocking to the other mamas, I know, because they are used to being quiet and obedient. Being a Bibi, I can get away with it! Age is respected here, and I will use it to my advantage, when I must!

That's the way the culture is here. Women are almost treated like servants. There are a few high-ranking female government officials, and the Tanzanian President, Kikwete, is promoting gender equality, which is promising. Of course, it will take longer for the culture to change in the 'bush.' But I hope my presence in Uhekule has been an encouragement to the women in the village.

CHAPTER THIRTY-SIX
Torch Day

To celebrate the independence of Tanzania from England in 1961, every year the government holds *Mwenge* (Torch Day). An entourage of visitors follows a 'torch' which travels through villages where structural improvements have been made. It's a way for government officials to observe the changes, thank the villagers responsible for the advances, and celebrate the great steps Tanzania has made towards bettering the lives of its citizens. It was going to be a great day for Uhekule because we were going to 'show off' the dispensary and the school library. The whole village was excited, and we began early to prepare for our important visitors.

The day was organized by the District Commissioner, the highest political office in Njombe. The District Medical Officer, the District Executive Officer, the District Education Officer, and some regional VIPS from Iringa would be following the torch that led to Uhekule. We expected about twenty-five people to arrive by bus for the presentation of our new buildings.

A month before Torch Day, we were scrambling to get everything ready. My experience had taught me that Tanzanians work slowly when they are not pushed or given big incentives. Igosi Vocational School was building our bookcases, tables and other furniture for the library, and they weren't working fast enough to ensure everything would be done before the big day. I gave them a deadline and told them I would deduct 5,000 shillings for every day they were late. Money talks, as they say, and the furniture was delivered on time.

Unfortunately, the varnish on the bookcases hadn't dried in time for the books to be placed on the shelves. There was no other option but to display the books on the library tables.

While I was working on the library, Dr. Ruanda from Njombe was busy setting up the dispensary. After months of my badgering, he had agreed to provide beds, drugs, curtains, and all the medical supplies we needed. He was working hard to make the dispensary look its best, and to be totally operational once we had staffing. That was proving to be more difficult than I had imagined, but 'if God wishes' was our prayer.

I worked for two hours arranging furniture and laying the beautiful books on the library tables. Too tired to eat, I took a lovely bucket bath, washed my hair, and got ready for bed. Tomorrow was the day, and I hoped I'd be able to get a good night's sleep.

That was not to be the case. Suddenly I heard a knocking at my door – it was the District Education Officer, who came to see how things looked before the big presentation tomorrow, and he wasn't happy.

He insisted that the books must be on the library shelves. He wanted me to move all the bookcases out to the veranda to dry. That way we could correctly display the books on the shelves tomorrow. I was exhausted and didn't want to do it, but he said he would lose his job if the books weren't set up properly. I do like this man, and I certainly didn't want him to lose his job, so I finally agreed. And he helped me move the shelves, along with the headmaster and another teacher, so I appreciated his willingness to help make it happen.

Earlier that day, the mamas jam group had come to me and asked if they could make a new batch of jam at my house. They wanted to sell some on Torch Day, which was a terrific idea, if only they had thought of it sooner! It showed a level of entrepreneurship, but not an iota of planning. I knew that I would be busy with the library all day, and not able to help them or even supervise. So, I told them a resounding "NO!" Then I left my house to work at the library and the mamas started making jam anyway! Now, when mamas make jam, there's chaos. When I came back home that evening, totally exhausted, I found that the house was a disaster. I'm sure the mamas were proud of themselves, (and, truthfully, I was, too.) But I was too tired to do much cleanup.

So, I finally went to bed that night in a messy house, totally exhausted from moving furniture all day, hoping the shelves would actually be dry enough for books tomorrow. The visitors were supposed to arrive at 10:00 am., so I would need to get up early to move the furniture back and place the books properly. It would be a short night.

And it was made even shorter when Molly, my sweet cat, decided to deliver her kittens at 3:00 am. And, of course, she chose my bedroom for her delivery room. That was the end of my sleep.

At 6:30 am, the headmaster Henry and another teacher friend, Jacksoni, were knocking at my door saying, "Bibi, are you ready for the bookcases to be moved into the library?" And so began my day and things were about to get worse.

The visitors were expected to arrive at 10:00, and we waited, and waited, and waited. Finally, about 11:30, the group arrived.

Their first stop was the library. Twenty-five dignitaries stood in the room listening as Dr. Ruanda gave a little two-minute speech. There was a quick tour of the library and the new classroom, and the group was off to see the dispensary. They were obviously behind schedule and running short of time because the division officer grabbed my hand, and we literally ran to the land cruiser and sped on to the dispensary. The ceremony there lasted less than fifteen minutes.

I was furious. Not one of our village workers received any recognition. I felt like the whole affair had been rushed. More time should have been allotted and the VIPs should have had more of a chance to look around. It had taken us months and months to accomplish what we had, and they gave us less than thirty minutes.

Maybe the best part of the whole day was that Molly delivered three healthy, adorable kittens.

Children in the library

CHAPTER THIRTY-SEVEN
A Robbery

I tried to get to Njombe town once a week. That's where I could get somewhat dependable internet connections, and I could correspond with my family through email. I also sent my monthly newsletters from the internet café in town. I wanted to connect with my supporters often, to let everyone know what projects I had been working on. There were many friends in the United States who sent funds for the dispensary or the library. There were others who sent books for the library. And still others had pledged to support students in secondary school. I wanted all these supporters to know how much good their money was doing. In addition, sharing the progress might encourage others to get involved.

On one of my trips to town, however, a bit of drama occurred in Uhekule while I was not there. I was robbed.

My house daughter, whom I love dearly, has a not-so-lovable brother. He decided to help himself to some of my belongings. I'm sure he knew I wasn't at home. I had a very large cart parked over by the school, outside the headmaster's home. This robber came right up and started to walk away with my cart. When some people witnessed the theft, they tried to stop him. A huge fight broke out with many villagers taking out their anger and indignation on this man. How dare he try to harm Bibi Kay? They came to my defense and took justice into their own hands.

It became pretty violent. In fact, if my schoolteacher friend had not intervened, I do think the man would have been killed. Fortunately, it didn't come to that. The criminal spent three days in jail until someone paid off a policeman to release him. That's another example of the corruption in the system of the country. We haven't seen him or heard from him so he must be in hiding somewhere. I think it's safe to say he won't be showing his face again in Uhekule.

CHAPTER THIRTY-EIGHT
In Search of a Doctor

We had a lovely dispensary, but no doctor. We had all the supplies and equipment provided by Dr Ruanda, but no doctor. We had plenty of sick or injured people, but no doctor. We had a beautiful home, provided by the government to house the doctor, but no doctor to live there. Time after time, we *thought* someone had agreed to come and staff the dispensary, but things always fell through.

Due to the shortage of doctors in Tanzania, we will probably have to settle for a medical assistant. Fortunately, we did have a nurse named Ngole. She had been with us for a long time and was actually quite knowledgeable. She would have to do for the time being.

The house the district built for the new medical staff person is really nice – bigger and cleaner and safer than my own house, which used to be the best house in Uhekule. This house is only a half block from the dispensary – a commuter's dream! I hope someone will come soon. I started asking for help in my newsletters to the states. Wouldn't it be wonderful if a retired doctor from the United States would come to serve in the dispensary for a year or two? Housing provided!

CHAPTER THIRTY-NINE
The End is in Sight

I had extended my term of service and would be leaving Uhekule on December first for Dar es Salaam. There were a lot of loose ends to tie up before then. Primarily, I wanted to assure that the money coming in for the sponsored students would be handled properly. I asked a friend of mine in Njombe if he would help, and he agreed. He is a very honest man, and I trusted him. Before I leave, I will open an account specifically for the tuition payments. He will continue to see that the funds coming in for the fourteen sponsored students would be correctly allocated, and I would get statements so I could oversee the transactions.

I was sponsoring three children myself. I felt so strongly that education was the best way Tanzanians could be helped. When I got to know these three children, learned of their hopes and dreams and saw their determination, I wanted to do what I could to get them through the next level of school. I believed that someday this poor society would have young people with knowledge to help Tanzania 'stand on its own two feet.'

As I made plans to return to the United States, I did so with a great deal of sadness. I was extremely happy with all the work that had been accomplished in my village, but I saw much more that could be done. Yet my term with Peace Corps was nearing an end. I had fulfilled my commitment to PC. But what about my personal commitment to my village friends? Leaving them would be difficult.

The villagers were beginning to understand that I would be leaving soon, and many questioned why I wouldn't just stay. I didn't see any way that would be possible without the backing of Peace Corps. I was told time and again, "If God wishes."

One day near the end of my term, I traveled once again to Njombe. As I got off the bus, I was greeted as usual by Isaiah, who was again selling his onions. But something was different this time. First of all, I noticed he looked sad and dirty. His usual smile was slow and seemed forced. Something was wrong. Then I realized it was a school day, and he should have been in class. I said to him, "Isaiah, this is Thursday. Why aren't you in school?"

His answer nearly broke my heart. He said, *"Mama kufa."* ("My mother has died.") I reached out and gave him a hug. Here was just one more orphan among thousands in Africa, and yet this one touched me so deeply. I saw the despair in his eyes, felt the anguish of loss and uncertainty, and knew that his future was bleak. I wondered what would happen to him, how he would survive, who would take care of him.

And I hated that I was leaving him.

The bus ride back to the village was, as usual, bumpy and uncomfortable. But I wasn't focused on the bumps and jiggles, I was thinking about Isaiah. My heart ached for him. I pictured the orphans in Uhekule, some living with aunts or uncles, some completely homeless, fending for themselves as best they could. Even those living with family members were often outcasts and treated poorly. I wished there was a better solution, a way to give the orphan children safety, security and a hope for a brighter future. Something was stirring within me.

Back home in Uhekule, the reality of my leaving was starting to hit everyone. Many villagers would come to me and beg me to stay. Many thanked me for my time and hard work. Many expressed sadness at the thought of life without me around. Huruma, the chief of the village, wanted me to stay, too. He spoke with me in all sincerity and said, "You can keep your house. You can have it. We give it to you. You can stay."

"But what would I do if I stayed?" I asked.

With only a moment's hesitation, Huruma said in Swahili, "Build us an orphanage, a home for the children who have no parents. The children need a place to live. This is what we need."

Suddenly the wheels in my brain started turning; everything looked clear – first my concern for Isaiah, now Huruma's plea. It all fell into place. An orphanage! Why, of course, that would be a wonderful project. It was definitely needed.

But how would I go about it? Without grants from Peace Corps, I would have to come up with funding somehow. I wasn't afraid of fundraising; I had much experience with that already. And construction of a building – I knew how to manage that, too. There was a lot to think about, but somehow it did seem like a possibility.

"If God wishes."

CHAPTER FORTY
Party Time

There was a lot of rejoicing when I told the villagers I was planning to come back and build an orphanage. My family back in the United States wasn't so sure it was a good idea, but once my mind was made up, I started making my plans.

I arranged to leave Uhekule on December 1 and go to Dar es Salaam for my close of service ceremony. There would be lots of final reports to write, summarizing all the projects I had been a part of. Peace Corps would also do a complete physical and dental examination, as well as some mental health check-ins.

My friend, Mike, would fly to Dar and meet me after the close of service. Then we planned to have a lovely vacation together, spending time mostly in Australia and Dubai. I let Mike plan all the details of our trip, as I really needed a rest and didn't want to be in charge of anything or make any decisions. I was looking forward to a peaceful time of rest and enjoyment. I needed some time to slowly acclimate into life outside of Uhekule.

The villagers threw me a going away party on November 3rd. I received many handmade gifts and a lot of food. The generosity of these people was overwhelming. Even though they knew I would be coming back in a year or so, they wanted to show their appreciation for all I had helped them accomplish. So, the gifts were actually 'thank you' presents, not going away gifts.

450 pounds of *mahindi* (corn) all shelled by hand
200 pounds of *ngano* (wheat)
15 pounds of *njegere* (dried peas)
27 (*yai*) eggs
15 *mikeka* (woven mats)
6 *pochi* (purses made of woven bamboo)
1 crochet doily
28 vikapu (baskets)
3 *ungo* (large woven trays)
1 *sahoni* (plate)
2 *vikombe* (plastic cups)
7 *kukus* (chickens)
3 *simbilise* (guinea pigs)
7 *vintenge/kanga* (cloth for dresses)
4 *mashahada* (lai)
1 beautiful suit from the teachers
9 African carvings
2 lovely greeting cards
1 *samaki* (dried fish)
9,200 shillings - $7.50 – I knew this was a big sacrifice.

I appreciated all these gifts, but since I don't eat guinea pigs, I promptly gave them away. The chickens I would leave behind, and my neighbors could feed them and gather eggs until I returned.

During this party, I was officially married. The ceremony was absolutely unbelievable, far beyond anything I could have expected. I became the bride of Uhekule. It was a special honor.

There were many guest speakers at the party, including the guest of honor, Mr. Lumato, the District Education Officer. He was a good friend, and I felt honored to have him at my big celebration.

Hundreds of villagers came to the party. In addition to the speeches, students sang songs dedicated to me. One of the songs was all in English.

My neighbors in Arkansas sent a video camera, and a kind Tanzanian friend filmed a lot of the party. I will always have reminders of this day. The party went on and on. Six hours later, we were still going strong and could have partied longer if the rain hadn't arrived.

In my house later that night, surrounded by gifts and reminders of the day, I thought back about my time in Uhekule village. The past two and a half years had been filled with adventures and learning experiences. I felt good about what had been accomplished. I felt positive about the changes and improvements. But in addition, I recognized that I personally had changed. I was stronger than ever before, and braver, too. I had confidence in myself, knowing that, even if there are difficulties ahead, God and I would be able to handle them.

As much as I looked forward to returning to the United States, and seeing my family, I knew I would miss many things about Africa. I will miss the quietness and serenity and beauty of this country. I will miss clean fresh air with no pollution. I will miss the simple life with no blaring televisions or invasive technology.

I will also miss being the smartest person around! In Uhekule, I am the most educated person, but back in Arkansas, I'm just of average intelligence! I will miss being treated like a celebrity in the village and in Njombe. Being the only white person, and an older one at that, makes me quite unique! I will miss the respect granted to all older people in Africa. Sadly, I think that will be different when I return to the United States.

But I also am looking forward to being back in the states. Hugs from my children and grandchildren will feel so wonderful. I can't wait to spend time with friends. There's so much to talk about! I also want to pamper myself a little with a manicure and a pedicure. And I was hoping to see some good movies in an air-conditioned theater. What a luxury! My love of movies and theaters began back when I was a child and continued still. I hadn't seen a movie in almost three years, and I was looking forward to it.

I started making plans for fundraising events. I sent out my last newsletter, asking for everyone to help me come up with speaking engagements, where I could talk about my hopes for the orphanage. I wanted to share my plans with churches, schools, PEO International Chapters, clubs or businesses. The more people learned about the sheer number of orphans and the great need for housing, the more funds I would raise. We had our camper back in Arkansas, and I could travel anywhere to speak.

CHAPTER FORTY-ONE

End of Service

In December of 2007, I spent several days in Dar, finishing up reports, reconciling the grant work and finalizing my exit from Peace Corps. There were medical visits, dental exams, and mental health evaluations. I had time to relax, regroup and focus on myself for a change! I had a chance to reflect on the things Peace Corps had accomplished in Uhekule, and I could look forward to the projects next to be done. I started thinking about the big job ahead of me – fundraising for the orphanage I wanted to build.

During these last days in Dar, I got word that Ron Tschetter, the director of Americans in Peace Corps, was meeting with Christine Djondo, the Peace Corp country director for Tanzania. They had been talking about me and my work! Ron had been the one who had suggested to David Monday that he should write a chapter in his book about me. Ron knew of me, but we had never met. When Christine called to invite me to lunch with Ron and his wife, I felt honored.

I was eager to meet with Christine, Ron, and his wife. and we had a lovely lunch at the PC headquarters. Ron was very interested in my work in Uhekule, and especially curious about the relationships I had made with the villagers. When I told him about my 'going away party' and shared about all the gifts I had been given, Ron was overwhelmed by the generosity of the villagers. He even asked if he could make a copy of my gift list.

When my time with Peace Corps was officially over, my special friend, Michael, came to meet me in Dar. We flew to Dubai and spent a week in that amazing city. Oh, my goodness, did I feel overwhelmed by culture shock. The elegance and prosperity were evident everywhere we went. Buildings, food, hotels, - everything oozed money. Men in long white robes walked proudly, heads held high. There was a feeling of dignity and power. Dubai has earned the nickname 'City of Gold', and it was easy to see why. Everywhere we went, we saw evidence of wealth. I wondered if any of the residents of Dubia had any idea about poverty and want. I wondered if any of them knew what good their money could do in a country like Tanzania. It would be transformed!

Then we flew to Australia and experienced another culture and way of life. Mike and I spent several weeks relaxing and enjoying time together. We spent Christmas in Australia and flew back to the United States in January 2008.

PART FOUR

BEING BIBI KAY

Chronic Africa

Chronic Africa
From "White Man Walking"
By Ward Brehm

A journalist was invited by friends to travel to Africa. He accepted the invitation, but as the departure date drew nearer, he became more and more apprehensive about the trip. When the day arrived, he went to the airport with every intention of canceling his plane ticket. Though his friends did their best to reason with him, the journalist seemed resolute in his decision. Then a shadow fell across their discussion, and standing tall above them was a holy man with an ancient, pointed beard and long black robes. The holy man addressed the journalist, saying, I have a word for you from God." The journalist, noticeably shaken by the man's presence, nevertheless asked him to continue. The holy man said, "You will go to Africa – and you will come back with a terrible disease." Hearing this confirmed the journalist's worst fears. The holy man went on to say, "The disease IS Africa. It will be in your blood for the rest of your life. And you will not be able to stay away." With trepidation, the journalist boarded the plane and went to Africa. And went, and went, and went – again, and again, and again.

White Man Walking
An American businessman's spiritual adventure in Africa
Ward Brehm
Kirk House Publishers, 2003

CHAPTER ONE
Back in the US of A

I settled back into my townhome in Hot Springs Village, Arkansas. Michael bought the townhouse attached to mine, which was very convenient. We could each have our own spaces, but getting together was easy, too.

I hadn't been home very long before I got a phone call from an editor at Peace Corps in Washington DC. He asked me to write up a story of my work in Uhekule Village for the inclusion in the Peace Corps book he was preparing for 2008. I was flattered but told him that I didn't have time. He interviewed me over the phone and wrote the story that appeared in the Peace Corps book published in 2008.

A short time later, David Monday called me from his home in Virginia. He said he was writing a story about his time in Tanzania and needed pictures so that the article could be published in the Wachovia Securities magazine. As an executive of Wachovia, he assured me that his company would send a couple of camera men and a costume and makeup lady to Hot Springs Village to take pictures for the article. These people were under contract with Wachovia and arrived at my home with camera equipment, clothes and makeup. It was quite exciting. Although my mind was concentrating on the big job ahead – fundraising for the orphanage we wanted to build – I was happy to spend a little time with this endeavor.

I had taken a few photos in Uhekule, and they were able to use them to illustrate portions of the article. They also wanted a picture of me for the cover of the brochure. I dressed in one of the kitangas I had with me, pulled my hair back, and put on an African beaded necklace. We went outside to a field with dried grasses, and the photographer took pictures. To look at the picture, you'd think I was standing in a wheat field in Tanzania!

David made one thousand copies of this four-page brochure and sent them to me. I was able to take them with me when I went to various places to talk about the orphanage. Armed with these colorful brochures, my fundraising began in earnest. Two friends in Little Rock and two friends in Hot Springs Village were very helpful in setting up speaking engagements throughout the state of Arkansas. Linda Rosinbaum and Yvonne Curtis arranged meetings at churches, Lions Clubs, book clubs and rotary meetings. Wherever people gathered, Linda and her helpers worked to get me in to speak.

I did a lot of traveling, sometimes alone and sometimes with Mike. One time when I was speaking at a church, Mike was with me. As I was describing the village of Uhekule and telling of some of the hardships the people go through just to survive, I noticed that Mike had tears in his eyes. He tried not to show it, but he was moved by my talk. Later the pastor spoke with us privately, and Mike opened up to him about his emotions. Mike had been overcome because he realized the differences between our country and Tanzania. He told the pastor, "We just don't understand how fortunate we are here. We live in the land of plenty, and over there, they have nothing."

We took our camper and traveled, with two other couples, to the Rocky Mountains. We camped and hiked through the Grand Canyon in Arizona. Every chance I got, I spoke to people about Uhekule. Some talks were arranged ahead of time at churches and clubs. But I even spoke to people I met at campgrounds! I was getting the word out, raising money and, in my free time, I was sketching floor plans for the orphanage. I couldn't get my mind off my friends in Africa.

Throughout that summer, I spent time with my family and visited with friends. I enjoyed an abundance of healthy food, the convenience of electricity and the luxury of long hot showers. Again and again, I thought about how fortunate we in the United States are. The poverty faced daily by my villagers can hardly be imagined by people who haven't seen it for themselves. I was making it my mission to teach about the many needs of Tanzanians.

My goal was multi-purpose. I wanted to share about what I had done with Peace Corps, and I wanted to stress the enormity of the needs that still remain. I was hoping to possibly inspire more Americans to become involved in improving the lives of my villagers and other similar places around the world.

Our dispensary still needed trained medical personnel. I spoke about this need whenever I had a chance. I wanted to encourage trained doctors and nurses to volunteer some time in Uhekule, or to seek out other places where their skills were so desperately needed.

I also tried to recruit sponsors for students who wanted to continue their schooling in secondary school, college or university. Most Americans were completely surprised to learn that a donation of only $1,000 could send a student to secondary school for a year. The cost of university was higher, (but still only around $2,000) and yet the American dollar would stretch so far. I was able to secure sponsorship for several students and had high hopes for how these educated young people would impact their Tanzanian villages.

I was actively collecting donations and pledges for money that would help with building the orphanage. Everywhere I told the story of my vision, people responded. The orphanage was starting to look like a reality. Those poor orphaned children, like Isaiah and so many others, would soon have a safe place to sleep and the promise of food and loving kindness.

During one of my presentations in Little Rock, I met a woman named Helen Porter. She was touched by my description of the hard work the village women must do to till their fields and plant their crops. She donated a huge sum of money and specified that it be used to buy a tractor that could be used to help anyone in the village. I was overwhelmed by her generosity, knowing how a tractor would ease the workload of so many of the Mamas. We could also use the tractor to break ground on the 60 acres given to the orphanage. It would be an asset when planting gardens for the orphanage children.

Not all of the donations were big enough to buy a tractor, but I wasn't discouraged. I remembered the Tanzanian saying, "If God wishes." Somehow, I knew God was with me in this endeavor, and I wasn't worried. And indeed, money started rolling in, slowly at first, but I never gave up. I was happy for every little dollar that was donated. I knew how far that dollar would stretch in Africa. Much could be accomplished, and life would be better for the children of Uhekule.

I traveled to California and gave a power point presentation to Paul Maloney and the officers at his silicone factory. It was well received, and the company was anxious to help bring solar power to my village. I had a suggestion, or maybe it was a request. Instead of supplying power to the dispensary, I pled for the electricity to be brought into the orphanage. I told the board about a tragedy that had taken place at a secondary school in another village. The students there didn't have electricity, of course, and were doing their studies at night by candlelight. One night, a student fell asleep studying. A candle was tipped over and caught the curtains on fire. The fire raged throughout the girl's dormitory, and several students died. I certainly didn't want that to happen in the orphanage. I was able to convince the officials that their donation of solar power would be better served if it was directed to the orphanage instead of the dispensary. Plans were made to send solar panels and all the equipment necessary to implement them to Dar es Salaam. The parts would be shipped from the US, which would take some time, of course, and stored in a warehouse until arrangements could be made for installation.

The mere thought of electricity at the orphanage was exciting to me. The convenience it would provide, as well as safety, was immeasurable. It would be such a blessing.

I started sending money to my friend in Njombe who had agreed to handle the finances for the orphanage. Fundraising continued through the summer, and I was pleased with the progress. As I made plans to return to Tanzania, I looked forward to being with my friends and doing great things for the children of Uhekule.

As I was busy making my travel arrangements, Mike came to me in confusion. "You're going back?" he asked. "I thought you'd stay here and send money, and they would do the work over there without you. I didn't know you were going back there." He was quite upset at the idea of me leaving.

I was a little surprised about his reaction. "Of course I have to go back. I can't just send them money. Who knows what would happen if I did that. I must go to make sure the orphanage gets built and things are done right."

I could tell Mike was perturbed, but I was determined. I had to get back to Uhekule, to make sure the orphanage would be completed properly. Mike said he wanted me to stay in Hot Springs Village and eventually we would get married. But, although the idea was tempting, I knew my heart was in that little village in the mountains of Tanzania. And I was disappointed that Mike didn't understand that.

After eight months in the states, I returned to Tanzania in September. As my taxi brought me closer and closer to Uhekule,

I was astonished at what I saw. Villagers were lined up along both sides of the road. They were waving and shouting greetings. Some put their hands together in front of them and bowed as I passed by. I was overwhelmed with emotions. I loved these people so much, and it was obvious that they cared for me, too.

CHAPTER TWO

Another Heartache

Shortly before I left Peace Corps, a man named Paskali, who was HIV positive, had come to me with his son and asked, "Why doesn't Juma grow?" This young man was nineteen years old, but very small in stature and weight. I asked the father if he would give me permission to take Juma to Njombe for testing. He agreed.

The following day, I took Juma to Njombe town to Angaza, a testing center. The doctor diagnosed him with stage 4 HIV. Immediately, he was a candidate for anti-retroviral medicine. So, he returned to secondary school in Makoga, and I traveled to the United States.

Eight months later, I was back in Uhekule and there was so much to do. I had a pile of mail to go through, and I didn't get to it right away. It was several days after my return that I found the letter that Juma had written to me. It was a plea for help. He explained that the boys in Makoga secondary school often teased him about his shrinking genital area, and he wanted me to take him to a doctor in town. I called Dr. Ruanda for an appointment for Juma on Monday. Unfortunately, Dr. Ruanda would be working in his avocado field that day, so the appointment was scheduled for Tuesday morning.

But on Monday, the day before the appointment, I was walking over to the primary school and encountered Nelson, one of the teachers. He asked me if I had heard about Juma. I shook my head and said I hadn't heard anything. "Juma fainted in class and was taken to Kibena Hospital in Njombe town where he died."

I was shocked and in disbelief. I knew he was taking the ARV medication, and I believed he was doing well. I quickly ran back to my house and the tears came. Had I failed him? If only I had read the letter sooner. If I had responded to his request for help quicker, would there have been a better outcome? Was I to blame? I realized he was in stage 4, but I felt responsible.

As I read his letter over, I struggled with grief and guilt. It was a low point for me. I had experienced death of the villagers before, but Juma's passing saddened me more deeply than most others.

CHAPTER THREE
First Plans

As hard as it was, I had to deal with my grief and move on. There was much to be done, and I wanted to get right to it. I met with the city council in Njombe. They helped finalize the floor plans for the orphanage. It would be designed to look like the school building from the outside, but instead of classrooms, it would have dormitories. There would be a boy's wing and a girl's wing, each with three rooms. Each room would have space for four sets of bunkbeds, so eight children per room. That would mean forty-eight children could be housed at one time. Each wing would have three *choo* (toilets) and three *bafu* (showers). There would be a centralized kitchen and dining space as well as a library and study area. The plan also included two septic tanks. Eventually a well with easy access to water would be included. And once the solar panels were installed, our orphanage would be complete – the most modern building in the bush.

We hired Ngoma, whose nickname meant drum, to be our contractor. He worked out the costs and finalized the blueprints. In 2009, the work began!

As with all construction projects, things have to be done in stages. Our tractor, purchased with funds donated by Helen Porter, was put to work clearing the land where the orphanage would sit. I was also able to buy a trailer in Dar. The day it was due to arrive, I was in Iringa taking a class in Swahili. I knew the truck carrying the trailer would be passing through Iringa on its way to Njombe, so I was watching for it. When I saw the truck, I jumped up from my seat in the outdoor class and ran to the road. I waved the truck to a stop. That truck would provide my transportation back to Uhekule. After a break for lunch, we were on our way. We rode five hours to Njombe, then more than one hour on very muddy roads the next day to Uhekule.

That trailer proved invaluable, as did the tractor, in the construction of the orphanage. The villagers got busy making mud bricks down at the river. Then our tractor pulled a trailer-load of bricks up from the riverbank to three huge kilns. The bricks were fired until they were set hard and usable for the walls of the orphanage.

The kilns were huge!

It was a long and slow process but would have been much more difficult without the tractor and trailer. Making 50,000 mud bricks was hard enough, but without the tractor, the bricks would have been carried to the kilns by hand. As it was, many of the villagers wanted to help and volunteered to carry bricks. Often the tractor passed villagers walking along the side of the road carrying five or six bricks, often balanced on their heads. But the villagers were invested in this orphanage project and wanted to be involved. I appreciated their willingness to help.

Everyone wanted to help – even if it meant carrying bricks
on her head.

One day, I was going to drive the Massey Ferguson 290 tractor, pulling a load of bricks to the kiln. As I walked to the tractor, I inadvertently stepped on a trail of *siafu* (biting ants). I didn't feel them crawling up my legs until suddenly there was a shooting pain in my genital area. The ants had crawled up to a warm moist part of my body and started biting. I jumped down from that tractor so fast, smacking my legs and digging at my clothes. All the villagers nearby began to laugh; they knew exactly what had happened to me. They took me to a home nearby where I removed my clothing and shook out all the ants. I checked carefully before getting redressed, and I vowed to look out for ant trails in the future.

As construction proceeded, I continued writing my monthly newsletter to all our supporters. I reported on the progress of the building, the excitement of the orphan children, and the need for continued support. I started requesting volunteers to come and help run the orphanage, once it was completed. We would need a housemother, a cook and someone to watch over the animals I hoped to raise for milk, eggs and meat. I made plans for a large garden, too, so the orphanage would never be without fresh vegetables. I envisioned good healthy meals for the children. I knew I would be directly involved with the operations of the orphanage, but I couldn't do it alone. I prayed for volunteers to come forth, good men and women who had servant hearts. I imagined that the empty dorm rooms could be used by the staff until the orphanage needed the space for more children.

CHAPTER FOUR

Construction Corruption

Construction of the orphanage took nearly two years. Ordering materials and having them transported from Dar took coordination and foresight. The general contractor, Ngoma, did a good job, but nothing in Tanzania is easy. Dealing with building supply shortages, transportation issues, and price-gouging corruption was a weekly drama. But eventually we got there.

The solar panels, along with all the installation equipment, had arrived. Everything was being held in a warehouse at the dock in Dar es Salaam. Getting the panels to Uhekule, however, proved to be more difficult than any of us had imagined. When I went to Dar to arrange for the transport of the materials, I was told that there was a duty on the equipment, and it wouldn't be released until the payment was made. It amounted to about $10,000. We certainly hadn't been told about any extra duty or tax that would be placed on our supplies. I felt this was a pure act of corruption on the part of the dock managers. There was no way I could come up with that amount of money.

Paul Malony got involved but didn't make any progress either. His company in California had donated the equipment and paid for all the transport. To have this additional fee tacked on at the last minute was unfair. Paul and I both felt the duty was pushed upon us because we appeared 'wealthy' and able to absorb the loss without much interruption to our business. They were sure wrong about that! We refused to pay the $10,000. In fact, Paul demanded that the wiring, batteries, inverter and connections all be returned to him in the US. He was unsuccessful in securing the thirty-two 180-watt solar panels, so they were left sitting in the warehouse, taking up space but useless without all the wiring parts.

I was furious. Our solar panels just sat there, and our dream of solar power for the orphanage was fading. I had already been in contact with a solar company in Dar that was ready and waiting to install the equipment, but so far, there was nothing for them to do because the panels were being held hostage.

Before long, I got a letter stating that I needed to pay 'rent' on the storage of our panels. They were charging $300 a day, and the panels had been there over a month. That was the last straw. I got myself to Dar as fast as I could and demanded to talk with the dock manager who was in charge. After several stall tactics, I began to wonder if my solar panels were even still there. Maybe they had been damaged, or even sold to another party. One of the office workers went into the warehouse to look for the panels and finally came back after half an hour and said he didn't know where they had been stored. With every minute that went by, I was getting more and more upset. But I wasn't going to give up. I wasn't going to leave until I had gotten some satisfactory answers.

One delay led to another, and I was there for two days before I finally got to talk with someone who could actually help me. I was about at the end of my rope! I shouted at the man in the office, "I don't know if you're waiting for a bribe or what, but you aren't getting a shilling from me. I demand to talk with your boss. Do you even know who your boss is?" Just then a well-dressed man came into the building, and the office worker nodded towards him.

I took off on a run (well, as fast as I could go) and caught up with the man as he was about to climb a flight of stairs. "I hear you are the boss," I said as I tried to catch my breath. "I want to know where my solar panels are."

"*Your* solar panels?" he asked in disbelief. "I just came across them in the warehouse and wondered where they were going and why they were still here. Come up to my office, and we'll figure this out."

In no time at all, I was explaining about the orphanage and the donation of solar panels, the duty tariff and the storage fee, and my desire to get what belonged to me and return to Uhekule. With a smile on his face, he waved his hand in the air as if he were chasing away a fly. "They are yours," he said. "No duty, no storage fee. Take them; they are yours."

I looked at him in disbelief. After two days of endless questions and demands, I was finally allowed to take the solar panels to my village. There was nothing I could do but cry. Tears of happiness streamed down my face.

Now there was a new problem – how was I going to move thirty-two heavy and breakable panels from Dar to Uhekule? The boss had a solution for that, too. He called his taxi driver and told him to bring a truck. "You are going to help Bibi Kay take electricity to her orphanage," he said. The driver was intrigued with this new assignment and didn't even charge a fee for the delivery.

I am not known to be an emotional crier, but at that moment, once again, I couldn't help myself. All the pent-up emotions of frustration, desperation and even anger gave way to relief and joy. The tears began to flow again. I was so grateful for the boss-man who was doing whatever he could to help me and by so doing was helping our children.

And in hindsight, I can say I learned a big lesson. If God wills a project, He will see that it gets done. It might not be on my timing, or in the way I plan or think it should happen, but it WILL get done. And ultimately, His plans are always better than mine!

In no time at all, the panels were loaded onto a truck, and we were on our way to Uhekule. The solar company from Dar was ready to start work. They supplied all the parts that would be needed as well as the technicians with the know-how.

Our next problem was where to mount the panels so they would catch the most sunlight. Once again, the answer came in a most astounding way! A Roman Catholic bishop in Njombe, Father Alfred Maluma, had used two large shipping containers for storage, but they were now empty. The bishop offered them to us and my friend, Fredy Mbilinyi, volunteered to move them to Uhekule. Fredy and his cousin brought the shipping containers into the village, and what excitement that stirred up! Before long, the solar panels were mounted on the tops of the two containers, and the solar company from Dar hooked everything up! The orphanage had electric power. It was like a dream come true.

So many times, over the years, I have seen miracles happen. From unexpected donations that provided books or tractors or solar power or sweaters or toys or shoes - the list is endless! And each time, regardless of the size of the gift, the items were appreciated and put to good use. It was satisfying to know that there are so many compassionate people in the world. As these good people came forth with their donations, I was reminded that great things can grow from small seeds. And I believed that great things were going to be growing in Uhekule. The lives of children would be changed because of this orphanage. And who could predict how those children would grow and what great things they would do in the future? I held on to hope.

Sunrise Children's Home
Uhekule, Tanzania

CHAPTER FIVE
Changes

I received an email from Michael, my special friend in the US. I sensed changes coming. In the email, he mentioned that some ladies from our hiking club had been 'smiling' at him. He asked me if I was okay with him seeing other women. What could I say? Here I was, thousands of miles away, fulfilling my dreams. How could I hold him back from pursuing his? I knew he was looking for a commitment, and I knew I was not in a position to grant it. So, of course, I agreed that he could date other women.

We continued to email each other. He was always interested in what I was doing, how things were progressing, and other news of Uhekule. He often praised my dedication to the villagers and expressed happiness at the good things that were being done. But things between us were different.

I planned to return to Hot Springs Village at least once a year, and I rather thought things would get back to normal once we were together again. Long distance relationships are always hard, but I thought the spark would be re-ignited in person.

CHAPTER SIX
Dedication

After the orphanage was completed, we got busy setting up the rooms. Beds and tables and chairs were donated or purchased. Kitchen equipment was in place, with tin plates and spoons for the children. Yes, spoons! I insisted that children in the orphanage should learn how to eat with spoons.

Some businessmen in distant towns wanted to help with the orphanage. They were men who used to live in Uhekule but had moved to towns and cities and started their own businesses. When they learned about what was happening in their home village, they got together and made plans to help. These men donated a cow and some chickens. Our children would have milk and eggs!

Each room of the orphanage was named after a benefactor. The names of people who had donated a substantial amount to the orphanage were painted over the doorways. I was honored to have my name painted above the library door. It did seem like the perfect place.

In 2011, the district commissioner and other dignitaries came for the dedication of the building. It was a special day, one that reflected the joy so many of us were feeling. From the villagers who had helped with construction, to the board of directors, to the children anxiously awaiting placement – everyone was excited. Mikaledi Mhagama, the new chief, and Anaye, who was a trustee, were so pleased to have fine buildings in the village.

Some of the Peace Corps Volunteers I knew attended the dedication. Many people from surrounding villages also came to tour the building. The orphanage was an important addition in the region and was of great interest to officials across the area.

Sunrise Children's Home was beautiful. The living conditions provided safety and comfort – far above what most of the orphans were accustomed to. To sleep in a bed instead of a mat on the floor – to have the promise of abundant, healthy food – to have running water and electricity – these were things most villagers could only long for. The donations and support of so many of my friends and contacts in America made this possible.

Henry, the headmaster of the primary school, began referring children to the Home. He had the best information about which children were in desperate need.

My efforts to recruit volunteers began to pay off. Through my monthly newsletters and the Sunrise Children's Home website, word was spreading, and soon we had the help we needed. One of our first volunteers was a Tanzanian nun who left her convent and came to help us with the children.

Without volunteers, we would not have been able to operate the home. Before long, we had young people coming from all over the world. Each of the volunteers brought a love of children and the desire to teach and encourage them.

Gerusa Ilha was a volunteer from Brazil. She stayed in Uhekule for two years. Others came from France, Austria and the US.

Two volunteers, Mark and Laura, came from Spain to work at Sunrise Children's Home. They were married in Uhekule. It was quite a celebration!

Two of my very good friends, who live in the Njombe area, are sisters from California. Chevy and Curry Anton were caregivers of a very large farm near Njombe town.

These sisters turned the farm into a place where young American volunteers could come to learn about 3rd world life. Chevy and Curry provided counseling and guidance while offering opportunities for camping and hiking, visits to welcoming villages and the opportunity to learn about the culture. Many of these young people were sent to Chevy and Curry by an organization in California called LEAPNOW.

The goal of LEAPNOW is to provide a work/study program abroad that will enrich the lives of young Americans. By sending them to remote areas, they could learn about different cultures. Many groups of these privileged young people came to Tanzania to learn about life in a third world country.

When these young people finished their time at the farm, a few of them wanted to stay in Tanzania and volunteer at Sunrise Children's Home. Several came through the years and most turned out to be great volunteers at the orphanage. We were eager to get their help and put them right to work. There was always kitchen work to be done, as well as caring for the animals and our large gardens.

Volunteers were making a difference in my village, influencing the children and setting good examples for the adults. But it was a mutual arrangement of benefit to Sunrise Children's Home and the volunteers themselves. As relationships grew and connections were made, lives on both sides of the ocean were changed.

Kay with volunteers and children

CHAPTER SEVEN
Back in the USA

I loved my time in Uhekule but found it necessary to return to the United States at least once a year. During my time back home in Hot Springs Village, I could reunite with friends, spend time with family, take care of personal business, and of course, attend more fundraising events. The Christ of the Hills United Methodist Church in Hot Springs arranged a videographer to create a YouTube video about the work in Uhekule. It was so well done and served as a marvelous introduction when I spoke at churches around the country. Titled "Mother of African Orphans," it can still be found on YouTube.

On one of my trips back to the states, I sat on an American Airlines plane with a young woman from California. We got to talking, and she was very interested in my work in Africa. All the way from London to New York, we talked about the children and the great needs in Uhekule.

This young lady, whose name was Corrinne Rice, was well educated and had a very good job. She was from California and had been in London for work. She expressed a desire to come to Uhekule and help me. I gave her my contact information and told her, "When you get your ticket, email me." Six months later I received an email from her. She was on her way! Corrinne stayed with us for two years. During that time, she received no salary but was given room and board. She proved to be an invaluable helper, and everyone loved her.

One time, while I was back in the USA, Paul Maloney invited me, again, to California to meet with the company that had donated the solar panels. I gave a presentation on the progress that had been made. Once again, Paul put me up in a nice hotel, and I appreciated my time relaxing and enjoying the beautiful California weather.

Another time, Paul came to Little Rock, and I met him at the airport. Then we took a drive to the home of Helen Porter. Helen had donated the money to purchase the tractor we so badly needed, and she was always interested in how things were going at Sunrise. She and Paul had a lot in common in that way. After a delightful lunch at Helen's luxurious home, she went to her desk and took out her checkbook. She wrote another huge donation check, then looked at Paul and said, "Oh, here, let's just add another zero!" It was a very generous amount, and I was extremely thankful.

* * * * *

Not all of my visits back to Hot Springs Village were filled with happy moments. On my trip home in 2013, Michael picked me up at the Memphis airport. He had driven my car from Hot Springs Village to Memphis because he wanted to spend time in Tunica. I thought we were going to stay in Tunica together and then go to our townhouses the next day. But I was a bit surprised to see that a female friend of ours, Linda, had driven Michael's car to the hotel and met us there. Mike told me goodnight and said we would meet the next morning for breakfast. I thought it a little odd but was tired from my long day of travel, so I retired to my room alone.

The next morning at breakfast, Mike told me that he and Linda had been married for three weeks. I was hurt, partly because he had found someone else and partially because he hadn't told me about it sooner. I knew that he was dating others, but he had never indicated that there was a serious relationship growing.

Somehow, I held it together as best I could and gave the couple my congratulations. But on the drive home to my townhouse in Hot Springs Village, I was in tears. I don't even remember the trip; all I felt was sadness and shock. As soon as I pulled into my driveway, I was greeted by my neighbor, George, from across the street. George and Nell Tatum had been my good friends for years, often sharing meals and outings with Mike and me. Now here was George, watching for my return, ready to lend comfort and a shoulder to cry on. He took one look at my tear-streaked face and said, "So, you know. I'm so sorry Kay." I collapsed into a sobbing mess, and he hugged me and patted my back. I immediately felt the comfort of that embrace. George and Nell helped me get through those hard days.

I was glad I had lots to do to keep myself busy. I had a trip planned to fly out to California, again, to do more fundraising with Paul Maloney and his company. Paul shared with me some books written by Dr. Paul Farmer, an anthropologist and physician who worked with underprivileged people. In 1987, Dr. Farmer and his coworkers had formed a foundation they named 'Partner In Health," He had started up a 501(c)3 to fund their work amongst the poorest of the poor.

Paul Maloney was intrigued with Dr. Farmer and the outreach of his foundation. He read several of his books describing work in Haiti, Peru, Rwanda and Russia. There was quite a bit of research done regarding the AIDS epidemic, and Paul knew I would be interested in Dr. Farmer's position on world health conditions. I could see that this man had a vision and compassion to bring better conditions to people all around the world. I returned to Uhekule with books to read and a new determination to recruit volunteers to help with the work.

CHAPTER EIGHT
Day by Day

A day in the orphanage began early with chores. Many of the children were still bedwetters. 'Potty training' was just something that wasn't taught by the adults. Culturally, young children did not wear any clothes below the waist. Bedwetting was typical in all of the homes, and in the orphanage as well. The bedwetters were responsible for washing their own bedding before going to school. The items were washed in a bucket of soapy water, then rinsed and rinsed again in clear water and hung out to dry.

After the students had cleaned the *choo* and their rooms, they dressed for breakfast. On the kitchen door was a list of chores that needed to be done and by whom. This list of workers would change weekly, and everyone had a turn. With no vacuum or cleaning lady, there were many chores to be done. We did have a cook, but the children would take turns helping to prepare the meals.

After breakfast, the dishes were washed and put away. Then the children would line up outside for 'inspection.' I checked their grooming and noted any health concerns. After that, we would have a group prayer and off they would walk to school, rain or shine.

There were chores after school, too. The village had given us sixty acres, and we used some of it for planting corn, potatoes, wheat, peas and beans. There were also huge gardens near the orphanage planted with cabbage, *figili, mchicha,* (local green vegetables), Chinese spinach, Swiss chard and carrots. We used these vegetables for our meals.

Our staff, the children and I planted the crops, fertilized and harvested. We also tended our avocado trees. It was certainly a group effort. Working together, the volunteers and I taught skills the children would use in their futures. It was hard work, but we knew it was important for the children to share in the responsibilities.

It wasn't all work around the orphanage, of course. Once the children knew they would be fed and cared for, they were able to find joy and have fun. It's interesting how mental health and learning go hand in hand. A well-nourished, relaxed child can learn. If he isn't worried about his next meal, or where he will sleep, or how he can stay out of the rain, he is more likely to concentrate in school and attend to his lessons. The children began to flourish. Their whole life improved; they found moments of joy where previously there had been hopelessness and despair.

Besides focusing on health and nutrition, responsibilities and education, I emphasized manners. I insisted the children should learn to use utensils at meals. No more finger eating or grabbing fistfuls of food at my table – oh no! We used spoons in the orphanage! But old habits are hard to break, and the children often automatically reverted back to their old ways. Whenever I would walk into the dining room, I would notice a few of the children glance up at me and immediately pick up their spoons and begin to eat. Their fingers were still messy with beans and rice, so the evidence was clear. They had been using their hands until I came into the room. But they wanted so badly to please me and were quick to show me they really did know how to use a spoon!

When Sunrise Children's Home first opened, I was the director. I took care of all of the administrative duties – fundraising, finding and training volunteers and staff and the day-to-day operations of the Home. Later on, we organized with a written constitution and a board of trustees. When I reached eighty years old, I was able to release some of my responsibilities to others. This allowed me to stay in the United States for part of the year and be in Africa only four or five months at a time. Eventually the Sunrise Children's Home was operated by missionaries from the US.

CHAPTER NINE

I Can See Clearly Now!

Every time I traveled back to the United States, I had speaking engagements scheduled so I could tell the story of Sunrise Children's Home. I continued to do fundraising wherever and whenever I could. But not all the support I raised came as a result of organized speaking engagements. Sometimes a casual conversation would lead to a whole new avenue of support.

On one of my visits back to the US, I had an eye appointment with Dr. Wallace in Hot Springs. During the exam, we got to talking. Dr. Wallace was interested in my African stories. I told him about an older village man who had cataracts so thick his eyes were white. "We really need you over there in Uhekule village," I told the doctor.

Dr. Wallace was so taken by my description of this village man, he decided to teach me how to examine eyes for glasses. Before I left his office, I was equipped with knowledge and a promise of several hundred pairs of reading glasses and other supplies to take back to Uhekule with me.

This was a greatly appreciated donation, and it came about just because I was sharing my stories of Africa. I certainly didn't plan on it, and it was completely unexpected. Talking about my children and the work in Uhekule came so naturally to me, and it often resulted in good things. These glasses would help so many school children. I couldn't thank Dr. Wallace enough. Even though he had not been able to actually travel to Africa and personally do exams for the villagers, he had found a way to help significantly. And who knows, maybe someday he will make the trip or encourage one of his colleagues to come. We might yet get professional assistance with eye exams. In the meantime, I knew a little bit about what to look for and what to do. And I had hundreds of pairs of reading glasses that would help.

After I returned to Uhekule, bringing all the glasses with me, I got to work. I was kept very busy examining the students in the primary school and village adults. To my surprise, one day a bus full of students from a nearby village arrived. Word travels fast in the 'bush.' Somehow, the teachers in the other village had heard that I had glasses that would help their students with eyestrain. So not only did Dr. Wallace's donation help my village, but children in neighboring villages as well.

And it wasn't just the children who benefited from Dr. Wallace's generosity. There was an adult man in the village who had compromised vision. He was not able to see well enough to read and always had to rely on others in the village to read to him. Fortunately, Dr. Wallace had included one pair of extremely thick glasses in his donation and, wouldn't you know it, they were exactly what this man needed. He put those thick glasses on and was overjoyed to see well enough to read again!

I vowed to keep talking about the needs in Uhekule wherever I went. I would never know just who would be prompted to help. As long as I had a voice, I would be spreading the word.

CHAPTER TEN
Floyd's Failing Health

I returned to the US in August of 2016, to attend my granddaughter's wedding. My ex-husband, Floyd, picked me up at the airport in Minneapolis. Although divorced, we had kept in contact with each other and had an amicable relationship. I noticed right away that Floyd looked ill. He was white as a sheet and had lost weight. I knew something was wrong.

Floyd said he had tried to make a doctor's appointment but wasn't able to get in. And he didn't want to go to the ER, even though I suggested that we should. He drove us to his townhome in Maplewood, and I was in for another shock. The house was in terrible condition. Every chair and table was piled high with books, papers and clothes. There was no place to sit without moving a stack of stuff. Dishes and carryout restaurant boxes covered the kitchen counters. It was obvious he hadn't been taking care of himself. There was no food in the house, so we went out to eat. I was very concerned about the environment he had been living in and worried about his health and future.

The next morning, Floyd finally agreed to get medical help, so I took him to United Hospital in St. Paul. He was passing blood rectally, which accounted for his pale coloring. They did many tests and within twelve hours, Floyd was diagnosed with esophageal cancer. They scheduled several appointments, and I stayed in Maplewood to drive him and talk with his doctors.

I took Floyd to a radiologist, oncologist and a surgical doctor to see what should be done for him. Floyd liked the surgeon we saw, so he chose surgery, and it was scheduled. When we met with the surgeon to discuss his procedure, the doctor asked Floyd, "Who is that lady sitting next to you?" When Floyd said, "She's my ex-wife," the doctor chuckled and said, "I've never seen an ex who was so devoted."

While Floyd recovered from surgery, I did what I could to clean up his townhouse and make it more livable. I knew I couldn't stay with him indefinitely, but I wanted him to be as comfortable as possible. After a few days in the hospital, Floyd was admitted to a rehab center. It was clear that he would not be able to live on his own. I stayed awhile to square away some of his financial business. He agreed to put me on his bank account, so I could pay bills for him.

Floyd gave me permission to sell his townhouse in Maplewood. But before it could be listed, it needed to be cleaned, and what an exhausting chore that was. I was able to contact some of Floyd's friends from AA, and they came and helped me. We took thirty boxes of books to the Salvation Army, including textbooks Floyd had accumulated from classes he had taken. We also donated clothing: fifteen pairs of khaki pants, some brand new, twenty pairs of black shoes and twenty of brown. Apparently, Floyd had never disposed of a bit of clothing. He had dozens of suits hanging in his closet, even though he hadn't worn a suit in many years. I took the suits to a resale shop that provided clothing for people interviewing for jobs. I hoped somebody would make good use of his clothes. I thought about the scant wardrobes of my villagers and remembered once again about the abundance of comforts in America.

Our daughter, Jill, came to help with the cleaning. Coming out of his bathroom, wearing gloves and a face mask, she asked me, "Mom, did he EVER clean that tub?" I was pretty sure he hadn't.

Some repairs needed to be made. A new sump pump was needed, and the refrigerator had to be fixed. I tried to clean the carpet because it was stained and dingy. The realtor said not to worry about it; the new owners would just gut the building and start over. So, the house was emptied and cleaned somewhat and listed for sale. I stayed a few days in Maplewood until the townhouse sold. It wasn't long until closing and all the business was settled.

We knew that Floyd would not be able to live alone, once he left the rehab center. Our children both had their homes, children, work and responsibilities, so neither of them was able to move back to Minneapolis to care for their father. I had my obligations in Africa and knew I needed to get back.

Our son, Jon, who was living in Columbia, Missouri, found an assisted living home that had a room for Floyd. He and his wife, Betsy, drove to Minnesota to get his father and settled him into his new home. After Floyd's townhouse sold, I returned to Hot Springs Village, stopping first in Columbia to see how he was doing in his new place. It was a lovely apartment at The Terrace, and I was thankful for the care they would be giving Floyd. Jon was nearby so he would be able to visit often.

I returned to Africa. It had not been a very restful time in the states, and I was pretty exhausted when I finally collapsed into my airline seat. Life in Uhekule was more appealing than ever. I looked forward to the slow pace and beautiful environment of my village. Compared to the stress I had just been through, Uhekule would be a vacation!

It wasn't long before I got word that Floyd was back in the hospital. He had been coughing for several days and was having trouble breathing. So, he was taken by ambulance back to the hospital. After a short stay in the hospital, he was again admitted to the rehab center.

While Floyd was in rehab, the staff noted that he was exhibiting signs of dementia. He didn't seem to understand where he was and would consistently ask, "Where did you put my bicycle?" He was not able to return to assisted living at The Terrace.

Jon kept in touch with me, telling me about the decline he was seeing in his father's health and cognition. In mid-February, Floyd was placed in hospice. He passed away on Feb. 19, 2017. I was still in Africa but had already made arrangements to travel back in March to attend a memorial service for Floyd.

As I thought back over our early marriage in Genoa, Illinois and our many homes all around the country, I was trying to focus mostly on the good times. We had lots of good memories and many wonderful friends. Floyd had worked for 3M for thirty-four years. He started in sales and moved to the Employee Assistance Program after he received his master's degree in counseling. He provided support to 3M employees facing difficulties in their lives. Whether work problems, family or marriage difficulties, or addictions, Floyd would get the people the help they needed. He even started a group to support gay and lesbian 3M employees. He helped many people with his counseling business.

Yes, there were demons and hard times. But all in all, we had come to terms with our choices and consequences. We remained friends even through our divorce. I still think of that handsome boy next door with fond memories.

CHAPTER ELEVEN
A Visitor in America

On one of my return trips to the United States, I brought a young Tanzanian man with me. Akiba Mgaya is one of the students I sponsored in school. Akiba attended Teacher's College and at the time of this visit, he was the headmaster of our primary school. He traveled to my speaking engagements and was a witness to all the good things that had been done in Uhekule, both through Peace Corps and in later years.

When he spoke before the congregation of my church, Christ of the Hills United Methodist Church, his testimony was engaging and well presented. He also left written handouts for the people to take with them, summarizing what he had said in his 'speech.' That helped people to understand him, since he did speak with an African inflection.

His words are reprinted here. It's good to read in a Tanzanian's own words the influence Peace Corps has had in the lives of one individual. Also, Akiba expresses thankfulness for education sponsors and appreciation for any funds donated to the orphanage.

Akiba Mgaya

A wonderful woman, Bibi Kay, came to Tanzania in 2005 as a Peace Corps Volunteer for two years. Within those 2 years, she built a library, office, classroom, dispensary and sponsored many students, about 40, in different levels.

For instance myself, I am one who got sponsorship from her to go to Tandala Teacher's College for two years. She helped me. Now I can say I am a good person. That is why we are still working together helping the orphanage. Without her, no life for me.

During her two years of Peace Corps, she conducted several seminars on health affairs, especially HIV/AIDS education and testing for HIV/AIDS after she knew that there are many people who are victims and orphans. She then built a beautiful orphanage.

The orphanage was opened in March 17th, 2011. Now there are 18 kids. Among the 18 kids, one is in Secondary School, which means she must live at a boarding school because in our village we only have education through 7th grade. The other 17 orphans are still in primary school in Uhekule Village.

At school, the kids are doing good in their examinations due to the beautiful environment of the orphans and the food they get at the orphanage compared to other students. One day, one of the teachers at school asked me what kind of food they eat at the orphanage because when they were living with their extended families, they were doing bad in school but now doing good. I told them to ask Bibi Kay which food does she feed the kids. In general, there is a big change in her kids.

However, I would like to thank everyone who attended here tonight making donations for the orphanage. Indeed, the kids need help as their parents died from AIDS. Also thanks for making donation for the workshop Bibi Kay plans to build soon. This workshop will be useful to the orphanage kids who do not pass the examinations. Also, the villagers can learn different skills from the workshop.

About me. Thank you a lot for warmly welcoming me to the United States of America. I appreciate your kindness.

I am married to Yusta, my wife, who is also a teacher and we have a 1 ½ daughter, Martha.

Starting last Monday, each day I am visiting Park Magnet School in Hot Springs to share the teaching experiences with the teachers at that school. I am having a good time sharing different experiences. Things are amazing to me at the school. On Monday and Tuesday, I spent the whole day in the kindergarten class. I will explain some of the differences.

1) Using computers and IPADS
2) How they participate in the learning activity
3) Asking questions
4) The class is active all the time
5) Teaching and learning materials
6) Learning Spanish

By seeing all the differences, I believe when I go back to Tanzania, I will make changes in several areas. For example, I am thinking to get one or two computers, a projector and printer now that the village will get electricity by this coming June. I hope this will help to start making changes.

Thank you,

Akiba Mgaya

CHAPTER TWELVE
More Success Stories

When I met Joina, she was just ten years old. As an infant, her hands had been severely burned in an accident at the cooking fire in her home. No professional help was provided for her, and she suffered terrible pain. Eventually, her fingers had fallen off, leaving her with just stubs at the ends of her arms. It was a tragic situation, and my heart ached for her. I decided she would need to attend a vocational school, to learn how to deal with her handicap. It didn't work out, so after a year at the school, I hired a lady to teach Joina how to use a loom to make baby clothes. With some assistance, she was successful.

One day I took Joina to see Father Maluma so she could show him the wonderful baby clothes she had made on the loom. When he saw the clothes, Father Maluma immediately bought all of them. Joina was overjoyed! She had earned 60,000 shillings that day (about $20) and had finally learned how to earn an income.

Joina with Father Maluma

A few years later, Joina moved four hours away to Iringa to live with an aunt. One day, maybe five years later, I had a knock at my door. When I opened it, there was Joina. She turned around and on her back was her baby. I was overjoyed. I am sure some man took advantage of her, but she was so proud and happy to have this baby to love.

During my Peace corps years, I helped to educate many young people. Joseph Mahagama needed financial assistance to become a teacher. He is now married with a family and teaches in a secondary school up in the Tanga area. During his earlier years of teaching, he would send money home for his mother and younger sister, Tumpe. Since Joseph was working, he was able to pay for Tumpe's college education. Tumpe's family is making a difference in Tanzania, thanks to Joseph's assistance. I am so very proud of them both.

Another one I helped was Beno Mgani. Beno went to a technical college to learn to be a pipe fitter. I found him a sponsor in the US to help with his school fees. When he graduated, the Tanzania Railways Corp in Dar hired him. His family in Uhekule was very poor, but Beno was able to send them money so they could replace their thatched roof with a metal roof and add a new room onto their house. I just love the 'trickle down effect'. I can help one, and he helps others. By passing on successes, one by one the lives of many were improved.

I'll never forget another story about Beno. He was a very ingenious young man! One day when he came home to Uhekule for a visit with his family, he asked if he could go to town with me. As I started up our orphanage Hilux pick-up truck, he hopped into the backseat. I drove to Njombe town, usually picking up a few others who were walking on the way. I asked Beno if he would need a ride home and he told me, yes, he would. We planned the time, and where I would find him.

After shopping, I called him to ask if he was ready for the trip back to Uhekule, and he told me where I could meet him outside of town. When I saw him and stopped to pick him up, he was carrying something wrapped in an old blanket. He got in the back seat, and we were off. A few kilometers down the road, I smelled a terrible odor in the truck. Finally, I asked Beno, "What is that awful smell?" It was not body odor, much worse. Beno unwrapped the blanket to show me the young pig he had bought for his father. I pulled over to the side of the road and ordered Beno to put that very smelly pig in the boot of the truck. Through the years, remembering that scene always produces a chuckle.

Several other students were assisted by sponsors who provided funds for their education. Yona is in Bible College, Hosea, Frankie and Nickson are attending universities, Sesilia is in Nursing School, Atukuzwe is in Pharmacy College and Halima is in Teacher's College.

The future looks bright for these students, and we can assume their villages and towns will benefit as well, as these educated citizens establish themselves and provide much needed services for their communities.

When Noel was an orphan at just six years old, I took him into my home, and we immediately formed a special bond. For twenty years, I have considered him to be my son. He is now in his last year at university in Arusha where he is studying law. His dedication to his studies and his desire to do good things is an inspiration. I'm so very proud of him, and extremely happy to have had a part in his education.

Shukuru and Leida were two of my many house daughters. Through the years, they have been a tremendous help to me, and I have been able to help them as well. Both of them finished secondary school.

Shukuru learned to do manicures and pedicures and now has opened her own little shop in Njombe. She is married and has two young boys. Her husband is a barber. They have been able to build a house of their own so they can move out of their one room rental.

Leida and her son, Gabriel, live with me when I am in my home in Tanzania. She mops the floors, washes my clothes by hand, and we cook together. She speaks good English and even little four-year-old Gabby has learned English from me. I am amazed at how quickly he picked up a foreign language, starting when he was just three years old. Sometimes he speaks Swahili with his mom and English with me.

I love that little boy! He is precious to me and can always make me laugh. One day, he had a bad cold and stopped eating. Leida was worried, knowing that he needed nourishment, and tried to 'force feed' him. She was trying to push a spoonful of food into his mouth, but Gabby kept his lips tightly sealed and refused to open his mouth. Finally, he looked at his mother and said in a loud voice, "Stop it! Stop it!" I had to laugh at his command of the English language! He got his point across!

One other success story involves the artist Chasaki, the man who painted the fetal development murals on the dispensary walls in Uhekule. In 2013, Chasaki earned a diploma in Arts from Bagamoyo College of Arts and Culture. He is now a well-known African artist. His paintings of village life, African animals, and mountain scenery have sold world-wide. Chasaki has a gallery of his paintings and also sells his work on-line through his website. Coming from a small village, using his talents and education, he has become a celebrated artist highly respected around the world.

CHAPTER THIRTEEN
Sad Stories Too

Every once in a while, I think back to Isaiah, the little boy who sold onions at the bus stop and helped me carry my packages. He was the inspiration behind Sunrise Children's Home. It was his plea for help that started me thinking about opening an orphanage. I'm sad to say, I never did hear what happened to him. I don't know if he found relatives to live with or if he survived on the streets. I never saw him again.

I realize that there are many, many children in Uhekule with needs. In other Tanzanian villages and other parts of the world, health and education are the keys to success in life. There are a multitude of places with no clean water, no electricity, no access to higher education. The needs seem overwhelming.

One person may not be able to *change* the world, but one person can *influence* the world for change. By looking outside ourselves, by finding ways to show love and compassion to those around us, by really seeing and listening to others, each of us can improve the world in a small way.

Organizations like Peace Corps have reached out to poverty-stricken areas and done amazing things to bring change and progress to those places. Other organizations, companies and individuals have joined together to provide for needs around the world. Opportunities exist still today – the needs are endless. All it takes is awareness and willingness. Be aware of the needs; be willing to give of ourselves. Everyone can have a part.

CHAPTER FOURTEEN
Retirement?

Every time I came back to the United States, people would question my plans to return to Africa. As I began to age (like everyone does!) I realized that traveling and responsibilities were taking a toll on me. I decided to spend most of my time in the states and only four or five months every year in Africa. I was usually in Tanzania from November to March, which is summertime there. It is never hot but always lovely.

I raised seventeen orphans in the ten years I was director of Sunrise. When I turned eighty-one, in 2021, I officially retired! Of course, the villagers threw me another party. With music playing and everyone in good spirits, they formed a line and offered me gifts. I'll never forget the big burly man who walked up to me carrying a goat thrown across his shoulders. As much as I appreciated his generous gift, I knew I could not take it with me, so I gave it to my neighbors for them to raise and then do as they saw fit!

Sunrise Children's Home would now be operated by missionaries, a married couple from the US. I would still oversee the finances and have an active advisory role. And of course, I would keep in touch with my friends and my 'children'. I continue my visits to Africa and stay in the Njombe area. I can reunite with the students I sponsor and catch up with all their news. I love hearing of their progress and success.

Currently, there are eight orphans in either college or universities. They are studying to become teachers, nurses, lawyers, pharmacists, preachers or graphic designers. Hopefully even more of the Tanzanian orphans will have the opportunity to go beyond grade seven.

I will continue to fundraise for Uhekule, seeking volunteers and sponsors for students. I will never stop spreading the word about the needs in Uhekule. I want to encourage more involvement between cultures, and I hope to inspire others to consider Peace Corps or other organizations that seek to make the world a better place.

Yes, I may be retired. But I'm not done.

Bibi Kay

Epilogue

As of this writing, I am planning my next trip back to Tanzania. I will spend my 85th birthday there, celebrating with my friends. I'm not sure how many more birthdays I have left, or how many of those days I will share with my African families. I do know that I count every day a blessing, and I am thankful for the opportunities I have had. My life has been full and complete.

I know that I have worked hard to make life better for my friends on both sides of the ocean. I have tried to share my knowledge (limited though I felt it was at times), and I have shared my talents and assets as well. My hope is that more people will be inspired to do the same. As I have tried to show in this book, even a small gesture of goodwill and kindness can be turned into big blessings for those in need.

Although my dream of joining Peace Corps wasn't fulfilled on a traditional timeline, I am continually reminded that there are many paths to success. I took a different path, but the rewards were great.

My time in Africa changed my view of life. I have become more aware of the needs of others, and I understand that one person *can* have an effect on the world. It doesn't take thousands of dollars or a lifetime commitment in a foreign country. Each of us is able to help others in our own way.

I would urge you to consider volunteering, either locally or globally, to encourage and support those less fortunate. Look at the opportunities offered through Peace Corps. Sponsor a student from an underprivileged village. Support a missionary. Serve at your neighborhood soup kitchen. Give money to service organizations helping after natural disasters. Get to know your neighbors who may not look like you or talk like you. Open your heart and your eyes. The needs are all around us. And take it from me, while you help others, you will find yourself changing and growing in astonishing ways.

I fell in love with the people of Africa. Ward Brehm, in his book "White Man Walking," called it 'Chronic Africa.' I caught the disease early and haven't gotten over it yet. Brehm says it best. "The disease IS Africa. It will be in your blood for the rest of your life. And you will not be able to stay away."

So, I return to Africa, time and time again. I urge you to find your own Africa – although it may be called by a different name. You might serve others in Nicaragua or Thailand or Ukraine. You might spend time with students at the elementary school down the street. You might find you can lend a hand at a homeless shelter. Whatever it is and wherever you find yourself, you will be changed.

Acknowledgements

I wish to share my utmost appreciation to my friend, Linda Rosinbaum, who agreed to read and edit my story. Your extra eyes were invaluable, and your encouragement kept me going. Thanks also to Bob Campbell, David Monday, Leida Mgeni, Mekio Mwinuka, and Noel Mgeni – your memories helped to stir mine! I want to thank Ward Brehm for his friendship and the use of his words. So many people have encouraged me to write this memoir, and I can't thank them enough.

Many 'kudos' to my good friend and the ghostwriter, Rosemary. We met in the spring of 2024, by chance sitting at the same table at a church function. Rosemary showed me the children's book she had recently published, and we talked about her four previous novels. I asked her if she would be willing to write my memoirs. This gracious lady said, "I have never been a ghostwriter before, but I am willing to give it a try."

After many meetings, phone calls and discussions, the book has come to fruition. All the time she was writing, she was also caring for her very sick, bedridden husband.

Rosemary is the type of person people always want for a friend; a kind, loving and generous gal, so genuine. I am very grateful to her and for her.

Thank you, Rosemary, for your time, dedication and love. KO

* * * * *

My thanks go to my husband for supporting my writing efforts and granting me time to work. Thanks also to Jerri Wood and Betty Gossell for their assistance with editing.

Most of all, thanks to you, Kay, for sharing your story and allowing me to have a part in telling it! I've loved getting to know you and I have been inspired by your vision. RJF

Additional copies can be purchased from the authors directly, from online booksellers, or through Riverview-Press.com.

Kay Oursler – kayhsv1@gmail.com
Rosemary J. Fisher – fisherrosemary72@yahoo.com

ALL PROCEEDS FROM THE SALE OF THIS BOOK WILL GO TO SUPPORT THE EDUCATION OF TANZANIAN ORPHANS.

Other books by Rosemary J. Fisher:

Under His Wings
Safely Abiding
Marked Safe
So Many Secrets, So Many Lies
That's My Sister